Exploring the Oregon Coast Trail

40 Consecutive Day Hikes
from the Columbia River to
the California Border

Connie Soper

DRAGONFLY PRESS

ISBN: 978-0-9768387-5-3

This book is dedicated to the memories of the great governors of the people of Oregon, Oswald West and Tom McCall, whose legacies live on. It is also dedicated with gratitude to the many friends and family members who supported and accompanied me on this journey. Most especially, it is dedicated to my parents, who first introduced me to Oregon beaches.

Contents

Foreword

THE OREGON COAST IS MADE OF ORDINARY WONDERS: ROCK, SAND, GRASS. Mixed among its many shapes are the headlands, coves, tide pools, and jigsaw jumbles of driftwood that delight us with every visit.

Governor Oswald West first had the vision to declare the beach a public highway in 1913, preserving its openness so we may visit it again and again without worry that it might be locked away for the benefit of a privileged few. In this last hundred years, people have rediscovered the coast in each generation, through a weekend camping trip, an afternoon of kite flying, or a walk on the beach.

The Oregon Coast Trail is one of the best ways for any Oregonian or visitor to this fair land to experience the same thrill that inspired Oswald West and every generation since. It serves us with both long and short walks in equal supply, delivering outstanding experiences to each person who takes the time to explore it. Whether you stretch your legs for days at a time or a few hours, there are everyday wonders in each mile. All you need is a friendly guidebook, a few signposts, and a sense of adventure.

If you've visited a hundred times or are preparing for your first journey, I know you will agree Oregon has done something precious with its coast that few states have even dreamed of.

—LISA SUMPTION, Director, Oregon Parks and Recreation Department, Steward of the Oregon Ocean Shore

As I went walking I saw a sign there
And on the sign it said "No Trespassing."
But on the other side it didn't say nothing,
That side was made for you and me.

Nobody living can ever stop me,
As I go walking that freedom highway;
Nobody living can ever make me turn back
This land was made for you and me.

—Woody Guthrie

Introduction

No Fences

THE OREGON COAST TRAIL (OCT) BEGINS ON SAND NEAR THE CONFLUence of the Columbia River and the Pacific Ocean and ends on sand some 400 miles later at the California border. In between, it traverses the length of the Oregon coastline, over half of it on the beaches. On any given day, those walking Oregon's shores will witness majestic waves rolling in, seastacks jutting skyward, and verdant hillsides extending all the way to those shores. They will see people building sand castles, riding horses, flying kites, painting, collecting shells, surfing, picnicking, exercising dogs, contemplating nature, or otherwise engaged in the myriad of recreational, artistic, or spiritual pursuits enjoyed at the seashore.

But there is one thing *not* seen on these beaches: fences. Oregon's beaches are public lands and, unlike in most other states bordering a shoreline, they cannot be privately owned or cordoned off.

The public's right to freely use all of Oregon's coastal beaches has resulted primarily from the foresight and political acumen of two Oregon governors: Oswald West, Oregon's fourteenth governor, and Tom McCall, Oregon's thirtieth governor. Under the leadership of Governor West, the Oregon legislature in 1913 declared the state's shoreline between ordinary high and extreme low tides ("wet sands") a public highway to be forever owned by the public. Oregon's Beach Bill, advocated by and signed into law by Governor McCall in 1967, allowed for recreational use of the dry sands area of the beaches. These stories are related in more detail within this book.

The majority of beaches in Florida are privately owned, such as this one in Palm Beach. (Photo by Jane Comerford)

The public's ability to use the entire length of the state's coastline is facilitated in large part by the proximity of public parks, waysides, or other points of access to the beaches—many of them acquired by Oregon's first superintendent of parks, Samuel Boardman. Today, sixty-six state recreational sites (slightly more than one-third of the entire state's park system) are located along the coast. Access to the shore is also provided at federal recreation sites, in county parks, or via city streets—Cannon Beach alone has identified forty-four places to get onto the beach. In total, there are 746 public access sites for 362 miles of coastline for the State of Oregon, resulting in access better than every half mile.

This Great Birthright

> Birthright: a right that you have because you were born into a particular position, family, place, etc., or because it is a right of all people

> —*Merriam-Webster Dictionary*

Nearly forty years after he had championed public ownership of Oregon's beaches by having them declared a highway, Oswald West wrote these words: "No selfish interest should be permitted, through politics or otherwise, to destroy or even impair this great birthright of our people." These words were reiterated by Governor McCall when he signed the Beach Bill in 1967. It is no coincidence that both governors, strong advocates for public access, held a great affinity for the Oregon beaches in their personal lives as well. Oswald West built a summer home overlooking Haystack Rock at Cannon Beach. Tom McCall owned a house at Roads End, near Lincoln City. What endures, thanks in large part to them, is our ability to fully appreciate and experience this great birthright by walking freely along all the beaches—beaches with no fences.

This is a book about the Oregon Coast Trail and is intended to serve as a practical guide for those who want to hike some or all of it. This book is also unabashedly intended as a celebration of our extraordinary beaches. For generations, people have come to enjoy the rugged and scenic beauty of these beaches, and they have come—and will continue to come—to walk. I suggest an itinerary of forty consecutive day hikes that collectively traverse most of the trail. Some people may prefer longer walks, especially if completing the OCT as a through-hike rather than a series of day hikes. Others may opt for shorter or less ambitious days on the trail. Not everyone will find it convenient to arrange for a car shuttle. The many public access points along the coast make it possible to improvise and, with sufficient planning, to create different options. With the exception of those hikes with tidal considerations, most can be structured as out-and-back ventures for those wanting shorter outings.

What is most important is to walk some of the Oregon Coast Trail—any of it, if just one day or one mile of it.

Walk the 804 Trail in Yachats, say, or climb up and over Tillamook Head along the same route traveled by members of the Lewis and Clark Expedition. Visit China Beach, deep in the heart of the Samuel H. Boardman State Scenic Corridor and only reachable by foot. Take in the same amazing views from atop Neahkahnie Mountain that greatly inspired the man who acquired the property on our behalf, Samuel Boardman. Hike through the three jewels of linked state parks near Charleston. Walk over and then under the elegant structure of the Conde McCullough–designed Yaquina

Bay Bridge. Catch a glimpse of whales breaching and spouting from the Whale Watching Center in Depoe Bay. Walk along the shore near Cannon Beach to Haystack Rock, knowing this was what Oswald West saw from his window.

What good is an inheritance if you don't use it? How can you best pass it on to future generations if you have not truly owned it yourself? For when the last grains of sand are emptied from your shoes, what endures is this: a great birthright and a walk well worth taking.

About the Oregon Coast Trail

A Unique and (Mostly) Beautiful Trail

THE OREGON COAST TRAIL IS UNIQUE BECAUSE NO OTHER STATE HAS DEveloped a trail along the length of its coastline (although California is working on such a trail). Technically, the Oregon Coast Trail is not a *trail* at all, since it does not provide for a continuous, uninterrupted path. But this is exactly what makes the OCT so special. While it does include wonderfully long stretches on the beaches, some portions wind through state parks or other public lands to take advantage of existing local trails and rights-of-way. It takes hikers on pastoral back roads, over headlands and capes, up forested trails, across historic bridges, down remote spits, and through the soft, sandy heart of the dunes. As such, it offers unparalleled scenery and a wild beauty experienced in personal and immediate ways.

Hiking the length of the trail provides an opportunity to explore Oregon's coastal communities by foot—Seaside, Gearhart, Cannon Beach, Manzanita, Depoe Bay, Winchester Bay, Charleston, and Port Orford, to name a few, are no longer just names on a map or places passed by on the highway. Some of these towns offer art galleries, espresso carts, and designer beers, while others seek to reinvent themselves, having struggled economically for years with the downturn of the logging industry. These towns are gems in their own right, and anyone with a modicum of curiosity about life beyond the tourist shops will find that curiosity rewarded.

OCT hikers trace the footsteps of the Native Americans who first developed and used these very trails, and they visit places of cultural and spiritual significance to those coastal tribes—places with names so melodious they roll off the tongue: Necanicum, Neahkahnie, Siuslaw, Yaquina. These places, too, evoke a painful past and darker side of Oregon's history.

Unfortunately, some 10 percent of the official OCT requires walking along the shoulder of US Highway 101 because headlands or cliffs prevent access to the beach, easements over private property are yet to be acquired, or there are no other trail options. The vast majority of these segments are eliminated from this guide because walking along US Highway 101, the major thoroughfare for the Oregon Coast, is unpleasant and unnerving and distracts from the overall hiking experience. Even where it is possible to walk inside a highway guardrail, which is not always the case, the terrain may be uneven and unsuitable for walking as well as strewn with broken glass, cigarette butts, and other debris—not to mention the roadkill.

OCT Maps and Resources

The OCT is managed by the Oregon Parks and Recreation Department (OPRD) as part of the state park system. Most of the lands comprising the trail, including the beaches, belong to or are managed by the State of Oregon, but other segments are federally managed or owned by local jurisdictions. In a few cases, public easement to the trail has been granted by private landowners. The OPRD has defined an "official" Oregon Coast Trail and provides a series of ten maps to illustrate the route, north to south; they are available only on the OPRD website.

In preparing to hike the trail for the first time in 2006, I realized no definitive guide was available. Several books, including Bonnie Henderson's *120 Hikes on the Oregon Coast*, Jack Remington's *The Oregon Coast Trail: Hiking Inn to Inn*, and William L. Sullivan's *100 Hikes/Travel Guide: Oregon Coast & Coast Range*, provided valuable information for some individual and well-defined segments of the trail. The brochure issued by OPRD was a good starting point, but for someone setting out on the ambitious venture of hiking the entire trail, it was incomplete. I should mention, however, that the brochure piqued my interest enough to complete the hike in the first place. OPRD's information has improved since publication of the original brochure, but the current set of ten maps still lacks enough detail on its own, and maps are not regularly updated when changes are made to the trail.

In the end, my hiking partners and I developed our own guide to avoid those stretches along the highway by conducting research and scouting the locations where each day's hike would begin and end. We prepared by poring over paper and online maps, talking to locals, and consulting with those who had completed some or all of the OCT. I hope to share what we learned—sometimes by trial and error—with others.

Why Hike the Oregon Coast Trail?

It has surprised me that many longtime Oregonians don't know about the trail, or that they confuse it with the more famous Pacific Crest Trail. But even if they are unaware of it, anyone who has taken a short stroll on the beach—any beach—in Oregon has most likely been on the OCT. There are many good reasons to hike the Oregon Coast Trail, whether for one mile or for the entire 367 miles as provided for in this guide. Here's the best reason of all: it's ours and we can.

The incredible and expansive scenic beauty experienced all along the trail is purpose enough for most people, and it is safe to say that anyone who reaches California by hiking the length of Oregon's coast will not soon forget the experience. It may not be any particular place or moment that is best remembered but rather the odyssey as a whole—the satisfaction of completing an ambitious goal, no matter how long it takes.

OCT travelers will better appreciate the difference one person or small group of people can make—whether it's an elected official using his position of power and influence in the best interest of all citizens rather than favoring the wealthy few, or a band of individuals working together to preserve public access to a trail steeped in history, or a journalist who used his craft to inform and motivate people to express their voices, or landowners generous enough to offer—rather than deny—access across their private property to provide a critical link in the Oregon Coast Trail.

Hiking the trail provides a unique opportunity to explore our heritage and to better connect with Oregon's history, even those chapters that are painful and difficult. While we cannot undo the injustices of the past, we can acknowledge them. The contributions of Governors West and McCall may be familiar to Oregonians, but it is important to tell them again, especially in the context of hiking the OCT. I hope to do them justice. Other stories—and the history of the coast is chock-full of them—are also interesting and important to know about, especially when passing through the very places those chapters of history were made. Who was Matt Kramer? Which lighthouse became a columbarium? How did the Hollering Place get its name?

Taking Time to Enjoy the Trail

Over the years, I have read and enjoyed numerous books written by women seeking adventure through extreme physical challenge—books, for example, about rafting a dangerous river in the Amazon, traveling solo through the outback of Australia by camel, or hiking alone along the Pacific Crest Trail. These women relate experiences of pushing through the limits of their physical endurance and the satisfaction of accomplishing more than they thought possible.

This is not one of those books. In my view, hiking the OCT is an experience to be savored with enough time and energy to contemplate and appreciate the surroundings, and it should not be considered an endurance test for the sake of finishing it.

Do not assume, however, that hiking the OCT is a cakewalk; some of the individual hikes are quite strenuous, and walking long distances on consecutive days, should you walk the OCT in that fashion, can prove challenging. But, for the most part, the route parallels US Highway 101, and you are never far from the nearest cappuccino or internet connection. With a few exceptions, the trail does not provide a wilderness experience such as, say, hiking the Pacific Crest Trail. Still, compared to those of other states (which of course have fewer public beaches), Oregon's beaches are not crowded or overly developed, especially in the southern part of the state. Therefore, it is quite likely that you will see few, if any, other people once passing even a short distance from a public wayside or parking area. On many days, you are likely to experience that wonderful sense of solitude and tranquility that comes from being alone on the shore, with no footprints but your own in the sand, and knowing those will disappear with the next rising tide.

History of the Oregon Coast Trail

Early Hikers

THE "FATHER" OF THE OREGON COAST TRAIL IS GENERALLY RECOGNIZED as Dr. Samuel N. Dicken, who was a professor of geology at the University of Oregon. He first proposed the idea of a statewide trail in a 1959 article, "A Hiking Trail the Length of Oregon's Coast?" published in *Old Oregon*, a magazine of the university's alumni association.

Dicken also wrote a book, *Pioneer Trails of the Oregon Coast*, which describes and illustrates trails established by Native American tribes (some of whom moved seasonally from place to place), by traders and hunters, and even earlier by herds of elk. He based the proposal in his article on knowledge and understanding of these early trails as reflected in his research and writings. In fact, hikers today traverse many of those same routes as well as some taken by explorers such as Meriwether Lewis and William Clark, or Jedediah Smith. Many times those routes took advantage of the hard and flat beaches.

Even before Dicken's proposal, Oregonians were enjoying the scenic coast and hiking it for fun. In perhaps the first written account of hiking the length of the Oregon Coast for recreational purposes, Guy Reynolds and his wife, Barbara, described their experience of walking the entire coast in a series of articles published by *The Oregon Motorist* magazine between October 1929 and June 1930. They stayed in inns and hotels along the way and kept a diary of each day's hike. Their writings reflect appreciation of the scenery and terrain they encountered, and they also provide directions and guidance for others who might want to complete the trek.

Not surprisingly (for this is a theme) the route they describe is similar to the trail today, although at times they bushwhacked or created their own trail, such as over Cascade Head (still a gap today): "The hillside is bare except for a little belt of alders in a gully near the bottom, and there is no trail, so just aim yourself at the aforementioned farm house and go as directly as possible to it....The farmer has a rowboat and some member of the family will no doubt willingly set you across Salmon River and coincidentally, into Lincoln County."

They report hitching rides from local fishermen or homeowners across rivers and bays, which would be so helpful today! These included Sand Lake, Netarts Spit, Nestucca River, Salmon River, and Siletz River. As the coastal highway and bridges had not yet been built, public ferries transported them across Alsea Bay, Umpqua River, Coos Bay, and other bodies of water. The Reynoldses did not carry cellular phones, GPS units, or titanium hiking poles, but they were equipped with a tide table and a great sense of adventure that transcends generations, as is evident in this passage:

> If you have not the spirit to appreciate the beauty and majesty of Nature, from the tiny frond of moss and fern to the thundering sea and the wide-flung vista of beach and forest, you'll be just a footsore, weary straggler along the way. If you have the soul that finds its sustenance in things like these, then every mile...will be a joy and an inspiration to you.

Some thirty years later, Dicken's proposal mirrored these same aesthetics and was practical as well, as he identified where new trail was needed and other challenges, including the need for water crossings and ways of navigating rugged headlands where there is no access to the beach. He further explained his rationale:

> Such a trail would make some of the more spectacular places, which only a few people have seen, available to the average hiker the year around. A traveler along Highway 101 has many opportunities to see the spectacular scenery in turnouts and even from the highway,

but many sections of highway are not close enough to the coast and even the new sections, relocated closer to the coast, are often in deep cuts because of the rugged nature of the country, so that much of the best scenery is lost to the person who stays on the road. A trail along the coast would make it available to all who care to walk a short distance.

He presented his idea to the State Parks Department, hiking clubs, and other groups to advocate for its development. The idea caught on with some elected officials as well. In a 1965 letter to the Bureau of Land Management, State Treasurer (and later Governor) Bob Straub expressed interest in and support for such a trail: "After we get the pollution cleaned up, the next thing I want to do is propose this beach trail from Washington to California. What ideas do you have on this? Can we call it the Lewis and Clark Trail with any degree of historical accuracy?"

Give Straub credit for vision, but less so for history, since Lewis and Clark never traveled farther south along the coast than what is now Cannon Beach.

From Vision to Reality

In 1971, the Oregon Recreational Trails System Act, intended to complement the National Trails System Act of 1968, was signed into law by Governor McCall. It required that bicycle and footpath trails be built and maintained wherever a highway, road, or street was constructed or relocated, and made provisions for trails in urban areas and near scenic areas. As a result, a State Recreation Trails plan was completed in 1979, and the first recreation trails coordinator, Jack Remington, brought on board. The Oregon Recreation Trails Advisory Council (ORTAC) was also established as part of the Recreational Trails System Act; its members were appointed by Governor McCall.

One of the council's first recommendations was to develop the Oregon Coast Trail. It was considered the council's highest priority because of the coast's unique characteristics and scenic beauty and because of the perceived potential to enhance economic development along the coast. As the first trails coordinator, Remington was charged with a wide range of tasks associated with building the trail, including negotiating easements, meeting with the public and other agency personnel, finalizing the details of the route, and overseeing trail construction.

••

Jack Remington recalls the early 1970s as a heady time for those concerned with protection of the state's natural resources. In addition to the Beach Bill's passage in 1967 and the Recreational Trails System Act in 1971, the Oregon legislature also enacted the nation's first container-deposit requirement (the Bottle Bill) in 1971, which required cans and bottles be returnable for a refund. In an era before comprehensive recycling programs, the Bottle Bill proved successful in reducing litter along the coast and in other scenic areas of the state. And in 1973 Oregon enacted land use legislation that established strict land use policies intended to avoid urban sprawl and to establish consistent planning and zoning standards throughout the state.

••

In January 1975, the Oregon Transportation Commission officially designated the first segment of the Oregon Coast Trail, 62 miles from the Columbia River to Tillamook Bay. Of those 62 miles, about 20 miles were newly built trail primarily through Oswald West State Park, south of Arch Cape and over Neahkahnie Mountain. Some labor was provided from the MacLaren School for Boys; in fact, penal labor is still used for building and maintaining trails. In July 1975, that segment of the trail was dedicated by Governor Straub, and Dicken cut the ceremonial ribbon made of foliage. At the time, it was estimated the entire trail would be completed within eight years.

In the article proposing the trail, Samuel Dicken wrote of his personal experiences hiking the southern coast: "The last part of this coast which I traversed was in the vicinity of the Natural Bridge, a striking feature which even today is little known to the people of Oregon." A memorial plaque in recognition of Dicken's founding the trail is located at Natural Bridges, which you will visit when hiking through the Samuel H. Boardman State Scenic Corridor.

How to Hike the Oregon Coast Trail

Purist or Pragmatist?

THERE IS NO ONE CORRECT WAY TO HIKE THE OREGON COAST TRAIL. YOU can complete it as an uninterrupted through-hike by carrying a backpack and camping or staying in motels along the way, or by walking it in segments over a longer period of time. While you can walk the length of the entire Oregon Coast, significant sections of it are along the shoulder of US Highway 101 which, for obvious reasons, is not as scenic or relaxing.

You will need to decide, then, whether to adopt the purist approach, meaning you will hike the entire trail, even those portions that include highway walking, or whether you prefer the pragmatist approach, which will result in eliminating segments of the trail in order to avoid the highway.

This guide adopts the latter philosophy. Wherever possible, it guides hikers to attempt to circumvent the highway, but some minimal shoulder walking is necessary, for example, to connect stretches of beaches separated by cliffs or headlands, or to get from one town to another. A description is provided of the conditions, because some areas are better suited for walking than others. In my view, those portions of the hike that are composed of significant stretches (more than one mile) of highway walking are not worth the unpleasant conditions and are therefore usually recommended to be avoided and are not included in the hikes. As a result, 45.5 miles, or more than 10 percent of the official OCT, is excluded from this guide, but these sections are called out here for those wishing to complete them anyway. Those portions of the trail along the highway that I recommended skipping include:

TABLE 1: OCT Segments Along US Highway 101 Eliminated from Guide

Area	Miles	Description
Barview Jetty County Park to Garibaldi Marina	2	This is a short but difficult stretch along the highway with no shoulder for walking.
Bob Straub State Park to Winema Road	6	Some of this gap includes local road walking, but more than half is along the highway.
Neskowin Beach State Recreation Site to Roads End State Recreation Site	7	This gap is in two sections because a Forest Service trail in the Cascade Head area eliminates some road walking.
Schooner Creek Wayside to Gleneden Beach State Recreation Site	3.5	This gap consists of unpleasant US Highway 101 walking.
Cummins Creek Trailhead to Muriel O. Ponsler Memorial State Scenic Viewpoint	6.5	This includes a difficult stretch of highway walking near Cape Perpetua.
Heceta Head Lighthouse State Scenic Viewpoint to Baker Beach Campground	4	Little or no shoulder exists along this section of the highway, which includes a tunnel with no pedestrian access.
Humbug Mountain State Park to Ophir Wayside State Park Rest Area	11	This is the longest gap and is mostly highway walking but has some beach access.
Pistol River State Scenic Viewpoint to Arch Rock Picnic Area	5.5	This stretch consists mostly of highway walking.

In other cases deviations are suggested to include hikes *not* currently part of the OCT, for example the Nestucca Spit (Bob Straub State Park) in Pacific City and the Sawmill & Tribal Trail in North Bend. Walking local streets in lieu of the beach is sometimes recommended in order to better experience some of the back neighborhoods of coastal towns.

Highway walking near Neskowin is especially difficult because of the narrow shoulder and lack of cleared vegetation next to the guardrail.

Trail Identification and Terrain

Official OCT signs are small metal placards usually attached to poles, but in some places wooden posts designate the trail. Hikers should be aware that the trail is not always clearly marked or otherwise consistently identified as the Oregon Coast Trail. Markers are rarely found on the beach, for example, so it is sometimes important to utilize other wayfinding techniques, such as identifying landmarks or using GPS devices, to know where to enter and exit the beach.

This guide suggests the OCT be walked as a series of forty consecutive day hikes beginning in Fort Stevens State Park and ending at the California border. These hikes are sometimes referred to by the order (day) they would be hiked (for example, hiking over Tillamook Head occurs on Day 3). Most of the individual day hikes included in this book are a combination of beach, road, and trail walking. Although this guide avoids most highway walking, about 1 percent of the terrain in this book's hikes

This is the official sign for the Oregon Coast Trail. More frequent and consistent signage would improve hikers' ability to navigate the trail. (Image provided by OPRD)

is along the shoulder of US Highway 101. It's important to note that *road* walking is distinguished from and different from *highway* walking. Road walking consists of traversing towns, usually on sidewalks, across bridges with pedestrian pathways, or along other side streets or roads with far less traffic than the highway.

When to Hike

The Oregon Coast Trail, or at least most portions of it, can be hiked any time of year, but Oregon's rain patterns may influence this decision. Western Oregon receives the bulk of its annual precipitation during winter. In fact, measurable precipitation occurs more than half the winter days, while in summer, only 10 to 15 percent of the days are wet. July is consistently the driest month throughout Oregon. On average, there is about one inch of precipitation in Astoria in July, compared to ten inches in December. Bandon's average rainfall in July is less than half an inch, compared to nearly ten inches in December. The most reliable good-weather conditions, then, are during July and August, but hikers should plan on using copious amounts of sunscreen as well as packing their rain gear, even in the summer. Certain river crossings may be more difficult or even impassable in the winter when water levels are higher.

Tides and Water Crossings

One of the more formidable challenges facing hikers of the Oregon Coast Trail is that of navigating the many water crossings. Most creeks, streams, and small rivers can be forded merely by taking off shoes and socks and wading across them. Some crossings, however, need to coincide with favorable tides. Other bodies of water—for example, Sand Lake, between Cape Lookout and Pacific City—can be circumnavigated. Some are crossed on bridges along pedestrian pathways. Many of these bridges were designed by Conde McCullough, and they are in and of themselves both practical constructions and elegant works of art.

As indicated in this guide, some hikes must be timed for low or lower tides. Sometimes the point (for example, a river crossing or rock outcropping) requiring access by low tide may occur several miles into the hike, so advance planning based on a projected hiking pace is required to estimate when those points will be reached.

Printed tide tables for Oregon beaches, based on separate tidal sites between Astoria and Brookings, are available at state park offices, information centers, and many shops and motels. They can also be found online at numerous internet sites, including one hosted by the National Oceanic and Atmospheric Administration (NOAA) at: www.tidesandcurrents.noaa.gov/tide_predictions.html.

In questions about river crossings, it's helpful to contact local park offices to learn about recent weather conditions that may impact your ability to cross a river. Crossing the New River (Day 31), for example, is not possible at high tide even during the summer and may not even be possible at lower tides if it has rained recently. You should also check with local parks personnel prior to attempting to cross the Sixes and Elk Rivers.

In some cases, while the hikes are not strictly tide dependent, meaning you can hike them at any time, portions of it may be more difficult at higher tides, and this has been noted in the hike descriptions.

Boats

This guide recommends using boats to cross bays or rivers on several occasions while hiking the OCT. Boat crossings are an integral part of Oregon's history because before the coastal bridges were built, travelers relied on formal or informal ferry systems to make connections between communities separated by water. Even purists would agree that taking advantage of boat ferries avoids many miles of tedious walking along the shoulder of the highway—and it's fun.

Ideally, boats would be used on Day 7, from the end of Manzanita Beach across Nehalem Bay; on Day 8, from Garibaldi Marina across Tillamook Bay to Bayocean Spit; on Day 9, from Netarts Landing across Netarts Bay to Netarts Spit; and on Day 22 by crossing the mouth of the Umpqua River into Winchester Bay.

At present, there is no formal relationship between OPRD and local marinas providing boat transportation. Establishing one would better incorporate water crossings as part of the OCT and would greatly facilitate logistics for hikers. Although no official relationship exists, the marinas at these locations are used to accommodating the needs of hikers and are usually willing and able to do so for a small fee. However, it is important to contact the providers ahead of time to make and confirm arrangements; some will have a set fee, and others will suggest a donation to cover costs. The crossing at Nehalem Bay (Day 7) need not be scheduled in advance, but the others do require advance planning, and the timing may depend on the tides.

••

Oregon Coast Trail Boat Providers
Contact information (as of 2015) for boat providers for each crossing is as follows; however, this information is subject to change and should be confirmed when planning the hikes:

- Day 7, Nehalem Bay: Jetty Fishery offers ferry service from 7 a.m. to 7 p.m. every day in the summer (and daylight hours other times of year). Call 1-800-821-7697 or 503-368-5746 once across from the dock.
- Day 8, Garibaldi to Bayocean Spit: Tillamook Bay may be crossed by calling 24–48 hours in advance to arrange for a ride, depending on availability, weather, tides, and other commitments. Garibaldi Marina offers the service; contact them at 1-800-383-3828 or 503-322-3312 for information about fees and schedule.
- Day 9, Netarts to Netarts Spit: The Netarts Bay Marina (503-842-7774) rents boats, but they do not directly provide transportation.

Your best bet would be to try to hitch a ride, informally, from the Netarts Landing County Boat Launch, but of course there is no guarantee of this.

- Day 22, across Umpqua River to Winchester Bay: Winchester Bay Charters offers and coordinates with other fishing guides to provide ferry service from 6 a.m. to 8 p.m. May 1 through September 30. Call 48 hours in advance to make arrangements for a pickup point. Phone either 541-361-0180 or 541-408-1128 for more information. This particular crossing differs from the previous two because the day ends, rather than starting, with the boat ride. Therefore, it is important to arrive at the designated pickup place on time. Missing the ride could result in backtracking some four miles to the nearest egress to the highway, which is at Sparrow Park Road.

Sand

It would not surprise me if coastal Indian tribes had as many words for *sand* as the Inuit have for *snow*, for there are many kinds of sand, some better suited for walking than others. In general, the beaches in the north, such as those near Cannon Beach, Manzanita, or Rockaway Beach, tend to be hard packed and excellent for walking—firm and solid beneath your feet. Farther south, the sand is coarser and sloped, and especially at high tide, walking can be a real slog. The sand in the Oregon Dunes is white and fine and granulated, and walking on it in August is like walking through hot sugar. You cannot avoid filling your shoes with it.

It's usually preferable to hike along the beach at or near low tide because more of the hard, wet sand beach is exposed, which is easier to walk on.

Where to Sleep?

The answer to the question of where to sleep depends on how you choose to tackle the OCT. My own experience was based on renting houses in different communities for weeklong stays. This approach allows for the convenience of carrying only a daypack and of the availability of a bedroom, kitchen, and hot shower each night. It also provides a unique opportunity to enjoy and get to know these towns along the way. This guide does not provide detailed information about camping or other lodging opportunities, but it is readily available by contacting the OPRD regarding campsites, yurts, or cabins at state parks or by contacting local visitor centers to arrange for a motel or house rental.

Food and Water

On most days, you are never very far from a town, park, or other facilities offering food, water, and other amenities. The walks in this book are intended as day hikes, so bringing a lunch or snacks along with a bottle or two of water should suffice. Some hikes, however—for example, the four days through the Oregon Dunes National Recreation Area—offer little or nothing in the way of supplies or amenities, and you should plan accordingly, especially to carry enough water.

Many of the hikes travel through or are adjacent to towns, so it is fairly easy to arrange for a lunch break or a coffee stop.

Gear

Because these are not considered backcountry hikes and you can complete all of them within a day, you won't need to carry a backpack with overnight equipment. You should, however, carry a few essentials in a day pack. These would include:

- tide table
- first-aid kit
- extra socks
- rain jacket or poncho
- sunscreen and hat
- water
- food

Some of the hikes include long stretches along the beach without shade or shelter of any kind, and weather conditions can also change without warning, so I recommend supplies for all weather conditions. Although a GPS is not really needed for navigation purposes, you might consider carrying one or another distance-tracking device because on some occasions (especially through the dunes) it is not obvious where to exit the beach, and missing an egress can result in backtracking and added mileage.

If you use hiking poles, they are most helpful for trail segments with significant elevation gain and loss, such as those over Tillamook Head, Arch Cape, Neahkahnie Mountain, Cape Sebastian, and Humbug Mountain. But poles can be in the way when walking long stretches on the beach or scrambling over rocks, so this is a personal choice.

Another personal choice is the kind of footwear to bring along. Hiking boots with ankle support are helpful for trail hikes, especially those that are muddy or prolific with tree roots. Walking sandals or lightweight athletic shoes are good for long beach stretches (which often involve crossing small creeks or streams) or for those hikes that combine beach and road walking.

Transportation

Because each hike in this book is point to point, two cars are required: one to transport hikers to the beginning of the hike and one waiting at the end. Depending on the number of people and the size of the vehicle, more cars may be needed. While the logistics of this approach may prove somewhat cumbersome, it allows for the convenience of a home base and the ability to complete a series of day trips from a central location. Furthermore, the distance between the hikes is not great, so a car shuttle is not overly time-consuming.

Alternatively, a volunteer driver could drop hikers off or pick them up, eliminating the need for a shuttle. In some communities, public transit or a taxi may be an option to provide services to or from access points along the OCT. Some planning and extra walking may be required, as the bus stop will most likely not be located exactly where the suggested hike starts or ends. You will need to refer to transit schedules, as service may be infrequent, not available on weekends or holidays, or seasonal in nature. In some cases, bus drivers have the discretion to make special stops or pickups along the route upon request or if previously arranged; it's worth asking about this. Each hike's description indicates whether using public transportation is possible.

Local transit agencies that provide services include:

TABLE 2. Public Transit Agencies Serving the Oregon Coast

Transit Agency	Telephone	Web Site	Area Served
Sunset Transportation Services	866-811-1001	www.ridethebus.org	Hammond to Manzanita
Tillamook County Transportation District	503-815-8283	www.tillamookbus.com	Manzanita to Lincoln City
Lincoln County Transit	541-265-4900	www.co.lincoln.or.us/ transit	Lincoln City to Yachats
Coos County Area Transit	541-267-7111	www.coostransit.org	Coos Bay and North Bend
Curry Public Transit	800-921-2871	www.currypublictransit .org	North Bend to Smith River, CA

Parking and Recreational Use Fees

There is no fee to enjoy any of Oregon's beaches. The state parks, waysides, and scenic areas that OCT hikers pass through can also be used without cost. Some coastal state parks, however, do charge a daily parking fee. These include: Fort Stevens, Ecola, Nehalem Bay, Cape Lookout, Heceta Head, Jesse M. Honeyman, and Shore Acres.

At federal recreation sites managed by the Siuslaw National Forest, a daily recreational use fee is required for those parking a vehicle. Those sites requiring a fee that you will visit along the way include: Sand Lake Recreation Area, Ocean Beach Picnic Area, Baker Beach, Oregon Dunes Day Use Area, John Dellenback Dunes Trailhead, and Horsfall Beach. A fee station may not always be located on-site, but payment is still required.

A long-term recreation pass is recommended if you are completing even a few days on the trail, as it is more convenient and cost-effective than paying by the day. The Oregon Pacific Coast Passport can also be purchased on an annual basis or as a five-day pass. It covers entry, vehicle parking, and day-use fees at all state and federal fee sites along the entire

Oregon Coast. You can purchase passports at all US Forest Service and Oregon Parks and Recreation offices along the Oregon Coast. Information about the pass is also provided on the respective agencies' websites.

Using this Guide

This guide describes a series of forty sequential day hikes that compose the OCT and is organized in four sections of ten hikes each:

- Days 1–10: Fort Stevens State Park to Pacific City
- Days 11–20: Pacific City to Florence
- Days 21–30: Florence to Bandon
- Days 31–40: Bandon to California border

Prevailing winds during the summer are north to south; therefore, it is recommended that the trail be hiked in a southerly direction, and the individual hikes are presented in this way. In most cases, each hike begins where the previous day's ended, although this is not always possible. Each hike stands alone and can be considered a pleasant day trip, or the hikes can be combined to complete the entire trail, excepting some gaps described in the table on page 14.

This guide provides information needed to navigate each of the hikes, including where each begins and ends, driving directions to those points, the trail's distance and elevation gain (if significant), tidal considerations, and a description of the route. In some cases, additional advance planning is needed, especially in arranging for boat trips and consulting tide tables. It is also helpful to plan each day's schedule to allow for a comfortable hiking pace and to take advantage of scenic detours along the way, and this guide notes those considerations.

One challenge in preparing a guide for the Oregon Coast Trail is that some hikers will prefer to log more miles per day than the average length of these hikes (9.2 miles) if their goal is to finish the entire trail more quickly, while others may opt for shorter hikes. With planning and consulting maps or other resources to identify access points (and, often, referring to tide tables), most hikes can be adjusted accordingly. However, as the hikes in this guide are designed to minimize highway walking, they often stop or start at access points intended to deliberately avoid it. As a result, it is difficult to increase the mileage without including stretches along US Highway 101. In other cases (for example, through the Oregon Dunes National Recreation Area), there are fewer opportunities to get onto or off the beach, making it difficult to shorten the hikes.

GPS coordinates are provided in WGS84 format for locations where it is helpful to locate a trail connection from the beach to a road that may not be immediately apparent.

Maps

Most hikes in this guide are illustrated with a mile-by-mile route map. The maps also illustrate the type of terrain and show route alternatives based on tidal considerations or whether a boat crossing is taken. For those hikes with significant elevation gain or loss, a corresponding elevation profile is provided. Points of interest and amenities, such as restrooms or parking, are also indicated.

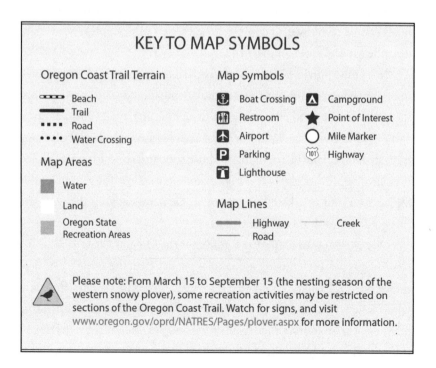

KEY TO MAP SYMBOLS

Oregon Coast Trail Terrain

- ▬▬▬ Beach
- ——— Trail
- ▪▪▪▪ Road
- •••• Water Crossing

Map Areas

- ■ Water
- □ Land
- ■ Oregon State Recreation Areas

Map Symbols

- ⚓ Boat Crossing
- 🚻 Restroom
- ✈ Airport
- 🅿 Parking
- 🗼 Lighthouse

- ▲ Campground
- ★ Point of Interest
- ○ Mile Marker
- ⑩⑴ Highway

Map Lines

- ——— Highway   ——— Creek
- ——— Road

Please note: From March 15 to September 15 (the nesting season of the western snowy plover), some recreation activities may be restricted on sections of the Oregon Coast Trail. Watch for signs, and visit www.oregon.gov/oprd/NATRES/Pages/plover.aspx for more information.

Safety and Disclaimers

This book is intended as a guide of suggested hikes and does not guarantee hiker safety. While for the most part, these hikes deliberately avoid long stretches hiking along the shoulder of US Highway 101, some highway walking is included. For those sections, use extreme caution because you will share the road with motorized vehicles, including large recreational vehicles, campers, and logging trucks.

Some hikes entail beach walking or river crossings that must be navigated at low tide, and it is therefore important that you plan the timing of the hikes accordingly. While this may prove challenging or even inconvenient, you should be aware of and never underestimate the presence of sneaker waves, rip currents, and the powerful undertow of the Pacific. More information on Oregon beach safety can be found on the OPRD website at www.respectthebeach.org.

While I have tried to accurately describe and map the hikes, it is very possible that your experiences will differ, or that you may encounter changes that have been made to the route. Hopefully, new links will be developed in the future to improve and expand the trail, but keep in mind that there is often lag time from when a new trail is built to when it is marked with signs. Although trail closures for maintenance are rare, portions of a trail may be closed for need of repair. It is therefore prudent to check with local park personnel to confirm which sections of the trail are walkable if you are in doubt.

Keep these caveats and cautions in mind and realize that, despite your best efforts at advance planning, you can't prepare for the unpredictable. You can't control the tides. You may not always immediately find the trail. But, like most great adventures in life, the beauty, inspiration, and pleasures you discover along this path are likely to come in unexpected ways. And come they will.

Summary of Oregon Coast Trail Hikes: Days 1–40

THE FOLLOWING CHART PROVIDES A SNAPSHOT OF THE FORTY HIKES, IN-cluding mileage and whether there are tidal considerations, and if so, whether an alternative route is available. It also shows where boat rides are recommended and whether arranging for public transportation to or from the trail is an option.

TABLE 3. Summary of Oregon Coast Trail Hikes

Day	Hike	Miles	Tide Consideration	High-Tide Option	Boat Crossing	No-Boat Option	Public Transit
1	Fort Stevens State Park to Sunset Beach State Recreation Site	9.7					
2	Sunset Beach State Recreation Site to Tillamook Head	11					X
3	Tillamook Head to Cannon Beach	9.8	X	X			X
4	Cannon Beach to Arch Cape	7.3	X				X
5	Arch Cape to Neahkahnie Mountain	9.3					
6	Neahkahnie Mountain to Manzanita	6.9					

Day	Hike	Miles	Tide Consideration	High-Tide Option	Boat Crossing	No-Boat Option	Public Transit
7	Manzanita to Barview Jetty County Park (with boat ride) or Manzanita to Nehalem Bay State Park (without boat ride)	11 or 7*	X	X	X	X	X
8	Garibaldi Marina to Netarts Landing (with boat ride) or Cape Meares to Netarts Landing (without boat ride)	12 or 8*			X	X	
9	Netarts Landing to Sand Lake Recreation Area	13			X	X	
10	Sand Lake Recreation Area to Pacific City	11 or 5**	X	X			
11	Bob Straub State Park	4.5					
12	Winema Road to Neskowin Beach State Recreation Site	5.5					
13	Roads End State Recreation Site to Schooner Creek	6.2					X
14	Gleneden Beach State Recreation Site to Devils Punchbowl State Natural Area	12.5					
15	Devils Punchbowl State Natural Area to Yaquina Bay State Recreation Site	9.8					
16	Yaquina Bay State Recreation Site to Seal Rock State Recreation Site	10.5					X

Day	Hike	Miles	Tide Consideration	High-Tide Option	Boat Crossing	No-Boat Option	Public Transit
17	Seal Rock State Recreation Site to Smelt Sands State Recreation Site (lower tides) or Quail Street to Smelt Sands State Recreation Site (high tide)	14.1 or 13.1 **	X	X			X
18	Smelt Sands State Recreation Site to Cummins Creek Trailhead	8.6					
19	Ocean Beach Picnic Area to Heceta Head Lighthouse State Scenic Viewpoint (low tide) or Muriel O. Ponsler Memorial State Scenic Viewpoint to Heceta Head Lighthouse State Scenic Viewpoint (other tides)	5.7 or 4.4**	X	X			
20	Baker Beach Campground to Siuslaw River North Jetty	5.5					
21	Siuslaw River South Jetty to Oregon Dunes Day Use Area	13					
22	Oregon Dunes Day Use Area to Winchester Bay (with boat) or Oregon Dunes Day Use Area to Sparrow Park Road (without boat)	13.7 or 7.2*			X	X	
23	Winchester Bay to John Dellenback Dunes Trailhead	9.5					
24	John Dellenback Dunes Trailhead to Horsfall Beach	11.5					
25	Horsfall Beach to Ferry Road Park	5.5					

Day	Hike	Miles	Tide Consideration	High-Tide Option	Boat Crossing	No-Boat Option	Public Transit
26	Ferry Road Park to Charleston	10.9					X
27	Charleston to Cape Arago State Park	7.5					
28	South Slough National Estuarine Research Reserve to Seven Devils State Recreation Site	7.1					
29	Seven Devils State Recreation Site to Bullards Beach State Park	5.5 or 8.1**	X	X			
30	Bullards Beach State Park to China Creek	8.7					
31	China Creek to Boice Cope County Park	12.9	X				
32	Boice Cope County Park to Cape Blanco State Park	7.3	X				
33	Cape Blanco State Park to Paradise Point State Recreation Site	5.6	X				
34	Paradise Point State Recreation Site to Humbug Mountain State Park	9.6	X	X			
35	Ophir Wayside State Park Rest Area to Rogue River North Jetty	9.9					X
36	Rogue River North Jetty to Cape Sebastian State Scenic Corridor	11.4					X
37	Cape Sebastian State Scenic Corridor to Pistol River State Scenic Viewpoint	5.6					X

Day	Hike	Miles	Tide Consideration	High-Tide Option	Boat Crossing	No-Boat Option	Public Transit
38	Arch Rock Picnic Area to Whaleshead Beach Picnic Area	8.6	X				X
39	Whaleshead Beach Viewpoint to Harris Beach State Park	7.9					X
40	Harris Beach State Park to Crissey Field State Recreation Site	8.9	X	X			X

*Hike distance depends upon whether boat ride is taken.
**Hike distance is based on tidal considerations.

DAYS 1–10

Fort Stevens State Park to Pacific City

Overview

In what can only be considered a very auspicious beginning to this great journey, you will begin hiking the OCT along the same beaches in Clatsop County that served as the focus of two legislative actions guaranteeing the public's access to the beaches in Oregon. In 1899 the state legislature declared the beaches of Clatsop County a highway, an action that resulted in ceasing the sale of tidelands to private owners; in 1913 that legislation was amended to include the entire shoreline. And, prompted in part by the actions of a motel owner in Cannon Beach (also located in Clatsop County) restricting the use of the dry sands to his customers, the Beach Bill was passed by the Oregon legislature in 1967. It guarantees public access to dry sands for recreational purposes.

The first ten hikes of the OCT offer a variety of terrain, starting with 16 miles of solid beach walking from Fort Stevens State Park to Gearhart. On the first day, you will pass by the remains of a shipwreck that occurred in 1906. On Day 2, you can explore the charms of Gearhart along the Ridge Path, which offers backyard glimpses of some of the town's cottages and gardens. Days 2 and 3 traverse the same paths and trails used by members of the Lewis and Clark Expedition through Seaside and over Tillamook Head.

Day 4 begins by walking along Cannon Beach, where you can see the reconstructed house once belonging to Governor Oswald West. On that same day, you will traverse Hug Point at lower tides along a rock shelf originally blasted out by early settlers to allow for stagecoach travel on the beach. The Oregon Coast Trail then continues over Arch Cape and Neahkahnie Mountain and into the town of Manzanita.

Three consecutive boat rides avoid long highway walks, and they are fun! Although using boat transportation is not officially part of the OCT, you can usually arrange these rides across Nehalem Bay (Day 7), and across Tillamook Bay to Bayocean Spit (Day 8). You may also be able to informally hitch a ride across Netarts Bay to Netarts Spit (Day 9), although there is not an official provider in Netarts. Alternatively, information is provided to modify the hike if you do not take a boat ride.

I recommend walking around Sand Lake rather than fording it, although, depending on favorable timing and your sense of adventure, you may be able to cross it at low tide in the summer. Once crossing Cape Kiwanda, you'll reach Pacific City and end the walk on Day 10 by standing at a quiet intersection where a highway expansion project was once envisioned. Bob Straub, Oregon State treasurer and later governor, led efforts to defeat the project, which would have paved over Nestucca Spit. It has since become a state park named for him.

Each hike picks up where the previous ended, except that, until a connecting path is built, 2 miles of highway walking between Barview Jetty County Park and Garibaldi are eliminated. Some highway walking is required between Gearhart and Seaside, and between Neahkahnie Mountain and Manzanita.

You'll pass through the towns of Gearhart, Seaside, Cannon Beach, Manzanita, Oceanside, Netarts, and Pacific City—each offers amenities such as lodging, restaurants, and visitor information.

Table 4. Days 1–10: Fort Stevens State Park to Pacific City

Day	Hike	Miles	Terrain	Considerations
1	Fort Stevens SP to Sunset Beach SRS	9.7	Trail, beach	
2	Sunset Beach SRS to Tillamook Head	11	Trail, beach, road, highway	

Day	Hike	Miles	Terrain	Considerations
3	Tillamook Head to Cannon Beach	9.8	Trail, road, beach	
4	Cannon Beach to Arch Cape	7.3	Beach, road	low tide
5	Arch Cape to Neahkahnie Mountain	9.3	Trail	
6	Neahkahnie Mountain to Manzanita	6.9	Trail, road, highway, beach	
7	Manzanita to Barview Jetty County Park or Manzanita to Nehalem Bay SP	11 or 7*	Road, beach	boat ride recommended
8	Garibaldi to Netarts Landing or Cape Meares to Netarts Landing	12 or 8*	Trail, beach, road	boat ride optional
9	Netarts Landing to Sand Lake Recreation Area	13	Beach, trail	boat ride optional
10	Sand Lake Recreation Area to Pacific City	11 or 5**	Beach, road	

*Hike distance depends upon whether boat ride is taken.
**Hike distance is based on tidal considerations.

Days 1-10: North Coast Overview

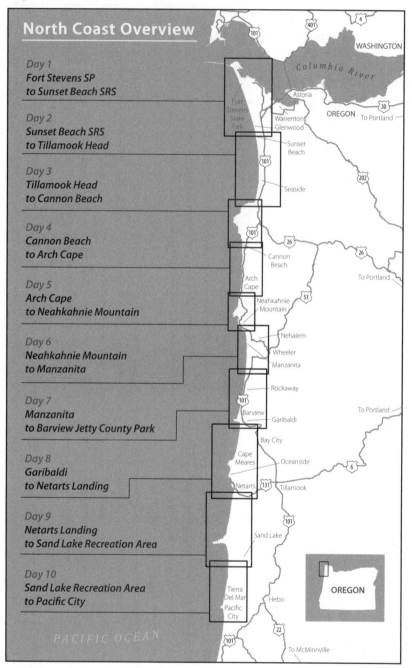

DAY 1

Fort Stevens State Park to Sunset Beach State Recreation Site

Distance: 9.7 miles

Terrain: Trail, beach

Begin: Fort Stevens State Park

Directions: From US Highway 101, turn west between mileposts 9 and 10 onto OR Highway 104 (Fort Stevens Highway). Veer left to get onto Ridge Road and continue until reaching Peter Iredale Road; turn left and enter the park. From there, follow signs to the Columbia River and then to Parking Area C at the south jetty. A day-use fee or pass is required.

End: Sunset Beach State Recreation Site

Directions: From US Highway 101, turn west between mileposts 13 and 14 onto Sunset Beach Lane and continue 1 mile to the parking area on the right. This is also the trailhead for the Fort to Sea Trail.

Overview

The first day begins at Fort Stevens State Park and ends almost 10 miles later at Sunset Beach. Except for the first 0.3 mile and the last 0.3 mile, you'll be on the beach the entire time. A highlight of this day is exploring a bit of Fort Stevens State Park and learning of its history as a military installation. You also pass by the remains of a shipwreck (the *Peter Iredale*) that occurred in 1906. And, if you intend to complete the entire Oregon Coast Trail, this hike launches a great adventure.

To shorten this hike, end it at the *Peter Iredale* shipwreck, about 4 miles into the walk, where there's parking if you leave a car. Fort Stevens State Park has an extensive network of bike and hiking paths to explore as well.

A soldier examines a Japanese buoyant mine, which drifted from Japanese waters to Fort Stevens beach between the *Peter Iredale* and the south jetty, 1945. (National Archives, Seattle)

At 4,247 acres, Fort Stevens is one of Oregon's largest state parks. The fort was originally built in 1864 to protect the mouth of the Columbia River from attack by Confederate vessels during the Civil War. It served as an active military installation until 1947. In 1942, the fort was fired upon by a Japanese submarine, which raised concerns that the West Coast would be invaded. Rolls of barbed wire were strung along the coast and around the wreck of the *Peter Iredale* in case of an invasion. The Fort Stevens incident was the only time during World War II that a continental United States military installation was attacked.

Fort Stevens became a state park in 1975. Land was given to the state by Clatsop County, and other parcels were acquired by gifts, leases, and purchases from the county, local school district, US Army Corps of Engineers, and a private landowner.

The *Peter Iredale* is entrenched in the sand shortly after the shipwreck, 1906. (Oregon Historical Society Research Library, ba006839)

Description

Begin the hike by finding the first Oregon Coast Trail sign just to the left of the viewing platform in Parking Area C of Fort Stevens State Park. Follow the sandy trail above the often roiling waters for 0.3 mile until the trail eases you down onto the beach. Head south and keep the ocean to the right. This walk is straightforward and unremarkable with the exception of coming upon, after about 4 miles, the skeletal remains of a shipwreck that occurred more than a century ago—the *Peter Iredale*. At low tide, it may be possible to walk around it.

•••

The *Peter Iredale* was an English four-masted steel sailing vessel headed for Portland from Salina Cruz, Mexico that ran ashore October 25, 1906. There were no casualties, and because little damage was incurred to the hull, plans were made to tow the ship back to sea, but after several weeks spent waiting for favorable weather and ocean conditions, the ship had listed and become embedded in the sand. It has remained there ever since.

The captain's final toast to his ship was: "May God bless you, and may your bones bleach in the sands."

•••

Remains of the *Peter Iredale* are still in the sand, 2013.

From the *Peter Iredale*, continue walking south for 5 miles. Nearing Sunset Beach, you might encounter cars on the beach. About 0.2 mile north of this egress on Sunset Beach Lane, which is indicated by a fluorescent chartreuse sign marked with the number *4*, look for a broad swath through the grass and walk through it to leave the beach. It leads to a wooden observation deck that may be obscured by low dunes. From here, follow the trail through the sand 0.3 mile to the parking area, where this day's hike ends.

Oregon's Beaches as a Highway

Sale of Tidelands

THE LONG STRETCHES OF BEACH WALKED BETWEEN FORT STEVENS STATE Park and Gearhart, and between Cannon Beach and Arch Cape are located in Clatsop County. You might be interested to know that, in 1899, the state legislature designated these very beaches as a highway, an action that set in motion the steps leading to a legislative declaration some fourteen years later that all of Oregon's shoreline be considered a highway.

When Oregon became a state in 1859, Congress granted it jurisdiction over all rivers and waters bordering the state. The State Land Board was then—as it is today—composed of the governor, the secretary of state, and the state treasurer and represented the state in matters involving state-owned lands, which include all tidelands. Beginning in 1874, the board began selling tidelands and conducted thirty-seven transactions that altogether sold about twenty-three miles of shoreline. Tidal lands were sold in each county bordering the ocean with the exception of Lane County. The first such sale, in February 1874, was for a parcel of 20.64 acres in Curry County, which sold for $41.28.

In 1899, the state legislature designated the shoreline of Clatsop County as a highway, an action prompted by these sales of tidelands to private parties, sales that could potentially restrict the use of the beaches for transportation by the public and that were needed for commerce.

The beaches had in fact long been considered trails and were used as a means of transportation first by Native Americans and later by those who settled in the area in the middle of the nineteenth century. Virtually all

Stagecoach travel was common along Oregon beaches. (Photo 316 provided by Lincoln County Historical Society)

of the long stretches of hard sand were used as roads, such as the beaches between Waldport and Yachats, Cannon Beach and Arch Cape, and the Siuslaw and Umpqua Rivers, among others. As white settlers, often lured by the promise of free land, moved into Oregon during the 1850s, they used these same routes. After stagecoach service was introduced, passengers commonly paid to take this transportation both on inland trails and along the beaches. Rivers and other natural barriers required the coaches to go inland or arrange for boat service, often provided by Indian canoes, across the water.

The first official county road designated by Coos County in 1854 was simply known as the Beach Route. The county board ordered "that a county road be established from Empire City to a stream known at the Ten Mile Creek.... And that appointed commissioners erect suitable monuments, to guide travelers and prevent accidents from quicksands on said road."

This route served as one of the main arteries of travel into and out of Coos Bay until the Southern Pacific Railroad arrived in 1916. It was not until the 1920s that a surfaced road was constructed in Coos Bay from the north to take the traffic away from the beach.

Governor Oswald West, center, poses on Nye Beach in 1912. He came to attend the Opening Fiesta of the season. (Photo 1545 provided by Lincoln County Historical Society)

Oswald West Elected Oregon's Fourteenth Governor

In 1910, the people of Oregon elected Oswald West as their fourteenth governor, or more accurately, the *men* of Oregon elected him, because women were not granted the right to vote until 1912. Only thirty-eight years old when he took office, West served as governor for four years. During his tenure, Governor West supported numerous progressive social issues as well as those related to natural resources. He championed, among other causes, woman suffrage (working directly with Abigail Scott Duniway in this effort), prison reform, and workers' compensation. But perhaps the achievement for which he is best known, and will forever be remembered and beloved by Oregonians, is that of convincing the legislature to declare the Oregon beaches as a public highway.

When asked by State Parks Superintendent Chester Armstrong how he got his inspiration for establishing the beaches as a highway, West sent a postcard with a picture of himself on a horse and the following text:

> Dear Armstrong,
> This is my old saddle horse, "Fred the Freak." I rode him from Elk Creek down Cannon Beach, and via Arch Cape over Neahkahnie Mountain mail trail to Nehalem. This was when and where I caught my inspiration.
>
> Your friend,
> Oswald West

At the urging of Governor West, the legislation specific to Clatsop County was amended to include the entire coastline. Senate Bill 22 was signed into law on February 13, 1913, and declared:

> The shore of the Pacific Ocean, between ordinary high tide and extreme low tide, and from the Columbia River on the north to the Oregon and California State line on the south, excepting such portion or portions of such shore as may have heretofore been disposed of by the State, is hereby declared a public highway and shall forever remain open as such to the public.

At the time, little public attention was paid to the legislation. The February 17, 1913, edition of the *Morning Oregonian* reported on the progress of the Twenty-Seventh Legislative Assembly, which enacted laws intended to: provide compensation for persons held as witnesses in criminal cases; make 100 pounds the standard weight for a sack of potatoes; prevent swine from running at large in certain townships in Malheur County; increase salaries of all circuit judges to $4,000 a year; and create a right of action against any person who gives or sells liquor to an habitual drunkard or an intoxicated person. It also passed SB 22, described in brief as: "Amendments making the shore of the Pacific Ocean a public highway."

Surely one source of inspiration for West's leadership in this issue was aesthetic and personal in nature. In 1913, West built a coastal retreat south of Cannon Beach complete with a panoramic view of the ocean, beaches, and Haystack Rock. West and his family enjoyed the house for many years, and it served as a place of respite and retreat. As reported by the *Daily Oregonian* on February 25, 1913:

> Governor West came quietly in from his place at Cannon Beach last night and left for Salem on the midnight electric.
>
> "I went down to my place to rest and grub stumps was all there was to it," he said. "And to tell the truth, I was so glad to get away from that bunch at the Legislature that I could hardly tear myself away today to go back to Salem… I may go away again tomorrow, if I choose to and if I do there will be no roughnecks around there breaking in my door to present bills at my office in my absence."

His Cannon Beach house was sold in 1936 and remained essentially the same as when West had it built until May 30, 1991, when the house was destroyed by a fire set by a sixteen-year-old arsonist. Over a period of eight years, the house was painstakingly reconstructed in the original style and was added to the National Register of Historic Places. It is located at 1981 Pacific Avenue in Cannon Beach and can be seen from the beach when hiking Day 4, between Cannon Beach and Arch Cape.

Governor West also recognized the importance of looking beyond the accomplishment of dedicating the beaches as a highway to ensure they could continue to be enjoyed and appreciated by the public. As he wrote in 1930, some fourteen years after he left office:

We have our Highway. There remains now anther task to make
complete the vision of the public-spirited men who set aside this
highway. Beauty spots along the highway must not be ruined by
private exploitation. Such spots, so essential to our program of
scenic development should and must be acquired by our state that
the foresightedness of the men who gave to us this strip of land be
not cheated by our own inactivity.

West did not run for reelection after his first term, opting instead to
move his family to Portland, where he practiced law until his retirement
in 1945. His home in Portland, located at 2559 NW Overton Street,
still stands. Oswald West died in 1960, two years after Short Sand Beach
State Park was renamed for him; his ashes were spread on Haystack Rock.

DAY 2

Sunset Beach State Recreation Site to Tillamook Head

Distance: 11 miles

Terrain: Beach, road, highway

Begin: Sunset Beach State Recreation Site

Directions: From US Highway 101, turn west between mileposts 13 and 14 onto Sunset Beach Lane and continue 1 mile to the parking area on the right. This is also the trailhead for the Fort to Sea Trail.

End: Tillamook Head Trailhead

Directions: From US Highway 101, turn west between mileposts 22 and 23 onto Avenue U in south Seaside. Turn left on S Edgewood Street and follow the road to its end. It will change names to Ocean Vista Drive and Sunset Boulevard, but continue straight ahead until the road ends at a small parking area for the trailhead.

Public transit is available via Sunset Transportation Services between Sunset Beach Lane (where it intersects with US Highway 101, 1 mile from the trailhead) and Seaside.

Overview

This hike combines long stretches of beach walking with town exploration by passing through two quintessential northern Oregon coastal communities—Gearhart and Seaside. You will view the backstreets of Gearhart along the historic Ridge Path, which was taken by travelers arriving by train from Portland into town at the beginning of the last century. And you will walk along the colorful Seaside Promenade, a boardwalk built in

You'll walk Ridge Path in Gearhart on Day 2.

the 1920s that runs through the heart of Seaside next to the beach. You will have to hike about 0.5 mile along the shoulder of US Highway 101, as it is the only link between the two communities.

The trail also literally follows in the footsteps of the Lewis and Clark Expedition, as evidenced by several historical plaques and other points of interest, including the Lewis and Clark salt cairns just off the Seaside Promenade, documenting their presence in the vicinity more than two hundred years ago.

Description

Begin the hike at the north end of the parking area, at the OCT sign next to the interpretive kiosk. Follow the trail through the sand and grasses for 0.3 mile to a low observation deck and return to the beach. Continue walking south for about 5.5 miles. Approaching Gearhart, look for any opportunity to leave the beach (often indicated by a pole or other directional marker) on any of the numerous trails leading through the grasses between the beach and the town, and find your way to 3rd

Day 2: Sunset Beach to Tillamook Head

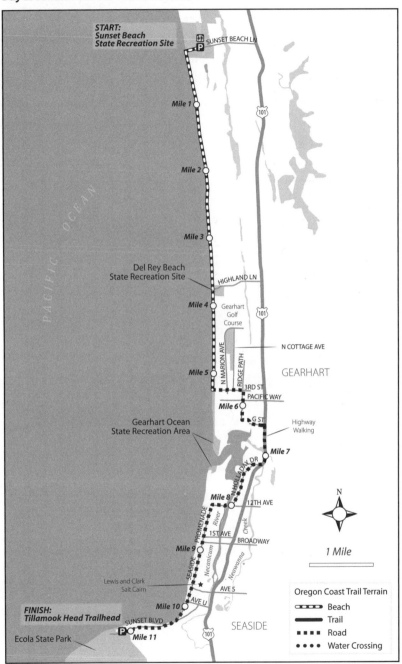

Street and Marion Avenue. GPS coordinates for exiting beach in Gearhart are: N 46°01.571', W 123°55.803'.

Walk up 3rd Street two blocks to the Ridge Path (which is clearly marked) one block east of Cottage Street. Take the Ridge Path south about 0.5 mile until it ends at F Street. The Ridge Path provides an intimate backyard glimpse of some of the many charming cottages and gardens unique to Gearhart that, for the most part, are hidden from view unless you hike the path.

In the early 1900s, fathers traveled by train to join their families at the seashore in the summer. Here is the "Daddy Train" in Seaside. (Oregon Historical Society Research Library, bb000459)

In the early part of the twentieth century, Portland residents traveled by boat and train to vacation in Gearhart and other coastal towns. Passengers would first take a five-hour trip via boat to Astoria and then catch the train headed south, which brought riders into the towns. During the summer months, mothers and children arrived and stayed for weeks at a time, while the men and fathers traveled on weekends. The railroad line became known as the "Daddy Train."

In Gearhart, a boardwalk near the station led to hotels, the beach, boardinghouses, campgrounds, or homes along Ocean Avenue, known as Gin Ridge. Homeowners along this stretch of beach would alternate hanging out a flag from their second-story windows, signaling to the neighbors which home was the destination for evening cocktails. The beverage of choice apparently was gin over ice, which is how the neighborhood got its name.

The mother of the noted American chef James Beard ran one of the boardinghouses. She cooked while James waited tables or helped in the kitchen. His culinary skills were influenced by the summers he spent in Gearhart, and he often returned as an adult to find respite from his hectic life in New York City and to teach private cooking classes in Seaside. When James Beard died, his ashes were spread over the beach in Gearhart. His family's house still stands on E Street.

• •

At F Street, head east a few blocks (it becomes G Street) until reaching US Highway 101. Walk south along the ample shoulder for a little more than 0.5 mile, crossing a small bridge over Neawanna Creek. Three streets—N Roosevelt Drive, 24th Avenue, and N Holladay Drive—converge at an intersection immediately after the creek crossing. Stay to the right of the traffic island and continue on 24th Avenue, and then veer left onto N Holladay Drive. Follow this road to 12th Avenue and then head west, crossing the Necanicum River, where locals may be crabbing and fishing from the bridge. Follow 12th Avenue until it ends at the beach, where the Seaside Promenade (the "Prom") begins.

The Prom is a concrete (originally wooden) boardwalk 1.5 miles in length that was built in the 1920s and is unique to the Oregon Coast. It is also possible, of course, to continue on the beach, but by walking the Prom you will be able to smell the caramel corn and better experience the essence of Seaside. You can also take a well-signed minor detour off the Prom between Lewis and Clark Way and Avenue S to see the salt cairns where members of the Lewis and Clark Expedition camped for six weeks in the winter of 1806, making salt to be used for preserving food.

Photo by A. M. Prentiss

The Seaside Prom was built as a wooden boardwalk in the 1920s. It is still a popular attraction. (Oregon Historical Society Research Library, bb012854)

Meriwether Lewis described salt making this way: "With the means we have of boiling the salt water we find it a very tedious opperation, that of making salt, notwithstanding we keep the kettles boiling day and night." It is difficult to imagine this activity would be any less tedious today. Nonetheless, on occasion volunteers in period costume reenact the process of boiling saltwater for the benefit of tourists. Check with the Seaside Visitors Bureau or the Seaside Museum & Historical Society for details.

Continue to the end of the boardwalk and get onto the beach at Avenue U. Walk the short distance south to the end of the sand, crossing over a bed of rocks and to the road. Follow Sunset Boulevard past the Lanai at the Cove motel as the path ascends about 1 mile (this is the only elevation gain of the hike) to the Tillamook Head trailhead.

Beaches Used for Transportation

THE DESIGNATION OF THE BEACHES AS A PUBLIC HIGHWAY IN 1913 AL-lowed for—in fact encouraged—the presence of vehicles on Oregon's beaches. This had already been the case since prior to the turn of the century, when there were no roads to connect communities along the coast. Beginning in 1893, stagecoaches traveled on stretches of hard sand to deliver mail and to transport passengers. Even when trains replaced some stagecoach routes, horse and buggy was a common way to traverse the coastline.

In the early decades of the twentieth century, automobiles became more prevalent, an occurrence that coincided with the development of the state parks system. More and more people came to the beaches by car for the same scenic beauty and recreational opportunities we enjoy today.

Inevitably, with the proliferation of vehicles, conflicts and concerns arose about safety. In 1947 the legislature directed the Highway Commission to designate sections of the beach where autos (and airplanes) were permitted and areas where they were not allowed. As a result, speed limits and other regulations were put into place. Still, the sands were populated with cars; in 1961, Cannon Beach estimated three thousand autos per day were on its beaches. Once the roads were built, the beaches were not needed for transportation, but people drove onto the beaches anyway to find a picnic spot, to otherwise recreate, or to park there.

In 1965, legislation was enacted to change the designation of the beaches from a highway to a recreational area to be overseen by the Parks

A horse and buggy travels in the surf at Netarts Beach. (From the collections of the Tillamook County Pioneer Museum)

A Model T Ford sits on the beach in Coos County, circa 1915. (Coos Historical & Maritime Museum, CHMM 992-8-0025)

and Recreation Department, which at that time was housed within the Highway Department. Cars were still allowed on the beach, but some towns (such as Cannon Beach, in 1985) petitioned the state to prohibit them.

Driving on the Beach Today

Today, driving street-legal vehicles on the beach is allowed only in designated areas and during specified times of year on about a fifth of Oregon's

A proliferation of cars caused congestion on Oregon beaches, such as on Nye Beach, 1936. (Photo 1975 provided by Lincoln County Historical Society)

Airplanes used the beaches for transportation as well. Two women pose in front of their biplane at Nye Beach, circa 1920. (Oregon Historical Society Research Library, bb012846)

coastline (Sunset Beach is one of those designated areas). Special permits for driving at other times and places may also be issued at the discretion of parks personnel for purposes such as gathering firewood, retrieving lost buoys or floats, or providing access for persons with disabilities. OPRD guidelines and rules spell out where and when driving is allowed, and these locations and seasonal constraints are illustrated on the official Oregon state map and included in Oregon Shore State Recreation Area Rules by county. These rules are available online at the Secretary of State's website at: www. arcweb.sos.state.or.us/pages/rules/oars_700/oar_736/736_021.html.

Over time, the public's attitudes toward cars on the beach have evolved. With rare exceptions the beaches are no longer needed for transportation. In a survey conducted for OPRD in 2002, the majority of respondents indicated that they do not want cars on the beaches at all; only 3 percent favored allowing vehicles on the beach with no restrictions. Of those who have operated a motorized vehicle on Oregon beaches, many indicated they did so "because it is allowed."

DAY 3

Tillamook Head to Cannon Beach

Distance: 9.8 miles

Terrain: Trail, road, beach

Begin: Tillamook Head Trailhead

Directions: From US Highway 101, turn west between mileposts 22 and 23 onto Avenue U in southern Seaside. Turn left on Edgewood Street. It will change names to Ocean Vista Drive and Sunset Boulevard, but continue straight ahead until the road ends at a small parking area for the trailhead.

End: Cannon Beach Library, 131 N Hemlock Street

Directions: Traveling north on US Highway 101, take the Cannon Beach City Center (Ecola State Park) exit between mileposts 29 and 30, travel west on Sunset Boulevard to Hemlock, turn right, and proceed 0.6 mile to the library.

Traveling south on US Highway 101, take the Cannon Beach City Center (Ecola State Park) exit at milepost 28, follow Fir Street (it changes to Elm Avenue and E 3rd Street), turn left on Spruce, right on 3rd Street, and left onto North Hemlock.

Parking is available in a public lot behind the library.

Sunset Transportation Services provides bus service between Seaside and Cannon Beach.

Overview

This hike travels over Tillamook Head, connects with a series of shorter trails leading above and through gorgeous Ecola State Park, and concludes with walking out of the park and into the town of Cannon Beach. While you'll spend little time on sand, the hike offers many panoramic ocean views all along the way. On a clear day, you can catch a glimpse of Tillamook Head Lighthouse perched on a small rock island over a mile out to sea.

The trail is believed to be virtually the same route used by members of the Lewis and Clark Expedition in January 1806 when they traveled with the guidance of their Indian scout and translator Sacajawea over Tillamook Head in search of a beached whale they hoped to use for food.

There is a total elevation gain of 2,150 feet and a total elevation loss of 2,236 feet. Be aware that the trail can be muddy and slippery any time of year, with many exposed roots.

This hike could be shortened by ending it at Indian Beach in the state park, where there is parking.

• •

Ehkoli is a Chinook word for "whale."

• •

Description

Begin by crossing a small bridge at the Tillamook Head Trailhead sign. After about 0.5 mile, the trail steepens and begins switchbacking up the hillside. The first 4 miles are a steady uphill climb, with most of the elevation gain on the hike in the first 2 miles. Then the trail goes up and down along the headland and through forestland lush with nurse logs, Sitka spruce, salal, and salmonberry. The trail is challenging because of many exposed roots, not to mention that even in the summer, conditions can be described only as a muddy, mucky mire that significantly impedes and slows the hiking experience. Occasionally, wooden boardwalks have been placed over the mud, but some are split or rotting, and where the mud is especially thick, you may be forced to walk off trail.

The ocean views, seen by peeking through the trees or at an occasional outlook, inspired William Clark to write on January 8, 1806: "From this point I beheld the grandest and most pleasing prospects which my eyes ever surveyed, in my frount a boundless Ocean; to the N and NE the coast

Day 3: Tillamook Head to Cannon Beach

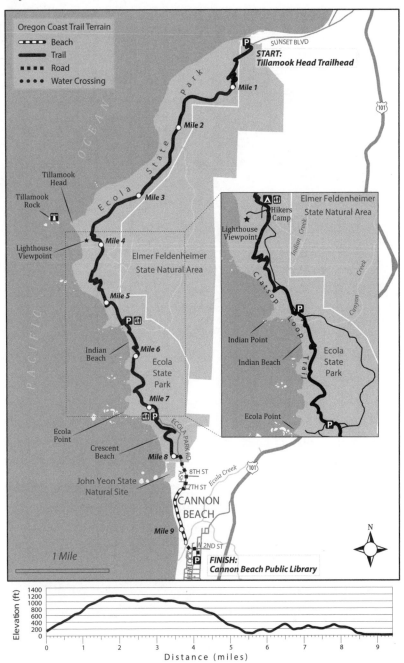

The Tillamook Rock Lighthouse was a desolate place. (National Archives, Seattle)

as far as my sight could be extended, the seas rageing with emence waves and brakeing with great force from the rocks."

And a most pleasing prospect it is.

On a clear day, you can see the lighthouse on Tillamook Rock in the distance, 1.2 miles offshore.

• •

Built on a small rocky island, Tillamook Rock Lighthouse is the only offshore lighthouse on the coast. It took three years to build under treacherous conditions and so was nicknamed "Terrible Tilly." The lighthouse was active from 1881 to 1957, when it was decommissioned and abandoned for two decades and then sold on three occasions to private owners.

In 1980 the lighthouse was renovated and converted to a columbarium, where interested parties could have their ashes placed inside the lighthouse, with prices varying from $1,000 for a place in the derrick room to $5,000 for a prime spot in the lantern room. Not bad, when prorated across eternity and considering the views.

However, the columbarium lost its license due to neglect and lack of oversight. It is still privately owned, and the island has been designated a federal wildlife refuge for common murres and cormorants.

The lighthouse, listed on the National Register of Historic Places, is visible on Day 3 from Tillamook Head and from Ecola State Park and is not open to the public. The Cannon Beach History Center and Museum sells books, photographs, and souvenir sweatshirts of Terrible Tilly.

• •

At 4.4 miles, the trail descends to a hikers' camp with small wooden shelters and an outhouse at a junction. To stay on the OCT, follow signs to the Clatsop Loop Trail, to the right. Going to the left, on a service road, will also get you to the same destination but is not as scenic. The Clatsop Loop Trail is fern-laden and lovely, and a welcome change after the mud. Continue to Indian Beach, where there are places to picnic and watch the surfers.

Cross the parking lot at Indian Beach and follow signs to Ecola Point, which you reach after 1.5 miles along a pleasant, undulating trail with multiple ups and downs, some of them quite steep. It follows a scenic bluff with many rewarding views and finally breaks out of the forest at the edge of the Ecola Point parking area. Cross the parking area and look for signs to Crescent Beach, next to the restrooms. Follow this trail a little more than 1 mile and turn left at the juncture, away from the beach, until it ends at Ecola Park Road. The going here is rough and steep in places, with wooden platform steps built into the slope.

Upon reaching the park road, turn right and follow it (with care, as there is little or no shoulder) 0.2 mile until reaching 8th Street. Turn right onto 8th Street and then make an immediate left on Ash Street. Where the paved road ends, follow the grassy slope downhill and then turn right onto 7th Street. At the end of 7th Street, return to the beach and walk 0.5 mile until reaching Ecola Creek, which can be waded at low or mid-tide. Once across the creek, take the set of stairs up to West 2nd Street, walk one block east to Hemlock, and turn right to reach the center of town.

If you get to the creek at high tide and can't cross it, head east along its banks a short distance to where you can access Les Shirley Park. Cross the park, turn right on 5th Street, follow it across the Fir Street Bridge, and enter town that way.

• •

In 1846, a US Navy schooner, *Shark*, was wrecked when attempting to cross the Columbia bar, and a small cannon from the ship washed ashore just north of Arch Cape. Finding the cannon inspired a name change for the small community—originally named Elk Creek and then Ecola—to Cannon Beach in 1922. The name change was prompted by the Post Office Department to avoid confusion with another town named Eola, where mail intended for Ecola was often sent by mistake. The Cannon Beach History Center and Museum is home to the original Cannon Beach cannon, and a replica of it is placed alongside the highway.

• •

The Beach Bill

Line in the Sand

WHEN THE OREGON BEACHES WERE DECLARED A PUBLIC HIGHWAY IN 1913, the legislation applied only to the wet sands portion of the beach, or the area between low and high tide. Most Oregonians, though, were under the impression they were allowed to have access to the entire beach, including the dry sands areas. The question as to what constituted legal public access to the beaches was finally challenged in 1966, when a motel owner in Cannon Beach erected a log barricade around his property and restricted use of the dry sands in front of the motel to those staying there. The owner intended to replicate a more exotic resort setting he had experienced in Hawaii by providing beach chairs and serving drinks to his customers in an enclosed area.

This incident generated public complaints and was brought to the attention of Highway Commission Chair Glenn Jackson and Parks Superintendent Dave Talbot. The motel owner claimed ownership of property to the high tide line, which was in fact reflected in his deed.

••

Events related to the passage of the Beach Bill are described in some detail in biographies of Governors Tom McCall and Bob Straub, *Fire at Eden's Gate* by Brent Walth and *Standing at the Water's Edge* by Charles Johnson, respectively.

Other accounts are available in two small books worth reading. They are out of print but can be searched for online. One, written by Kathryn A. Straton and published by the Oregon State Parks and

Recreation Branch in 1977, is titled *Oregon's Beaches, a Birthright Preserved,* and the other is Matt Love's book *Grasping Wastrels vs. Beaches Forever Inc.,* published in 2003 by Nestucca Spit Press. More recently, Ms. Straton, Mr. Love, and filmmaker Tom Olsen Jr. collaborated on a video accounting of the Beach Bill titled *Politics of Sand,* produced by the Cannon Beach History Center, which includes interesting interviews with numerous key players instrumental in the bill's passage as well as with some who opposed it.

House Bill 1601

The sequence of events that lead to the passage of the Beach Bill began with a recommendation by the Parks Advisory Committee to the State Highway Commission that legislation be explored to clarify the state's legal position regarding beach access.

New legislation was drafted based on the Texas Open Beaches Act of 1959, which allowed the public access to the dry sands area of Texas beaches based on customary use. In early 1967, House Bill 1601 was introduced, proposing public use of the dry sand beaches to the vegetation line based on the public's continuous use of those lands. The bill was referred to the House Highway Committee, where it was stalled for several months as committee members debated where the boundary for public use should be, because some did not support extending it as far as the vegetation line. Some coastal legislators did not support it at all, as their constituents feared losing property rights.

At first, the bill attracted little attention and might have died in committee except for several notable events. First, committee Chair Sidney Bazett, a Republican from Grants Pass, agreed to convene another public hearing on the bill. As a result, citizen activists were given more time to organize their support and to provide testimony. Second, the media began to focus on the issue. In an era before the internet and social media, people relied on—and were influenced by—newspapers and television accounts. In particular, a series of newspaper articles written by journalist Matt Kramer drew attention to the pending legislation. He is widely attributed with coining the term *Beach Bill.*

Governor Tom McCall poses before the Surfsand Motel in Cannon Beach with its log barricade, 1967. (Oregon Historical Society Research Library, bb005805)

In May 1967, KGW, a Portland-based television station, aired an editorial that opened with a photographic collage of Haystack Rock enclosed in a fence and went on to suggest that members of the public notify their elected officials of their support for the legislation if they did not want to lose their beaches.

This image resonated with the public, and over the next few weeks, some forty thousand letters, telegrams, or other means of communication were directed to the committee or Governor McCall, the vast majority favoring public access to the dry sand beaches. No issue in Oregon history before or since has generated such extensive public response.

On May 13, Governor McCall personally visited five beaches with a team of surveyors in order to call attention to the legislation and to visually display where the boundary would be at the proposed sixteen feet above sea level (roughly equivalent to the vegetation line). In a particularly dramatic manner, he toured the beaches via helicopter.

The committee continued to refine the bill and ultimately brought it to a vote. The legislation, written with public access allowed to the vegetation line, passed the House and Senate and was signed into law by Governor McCall on July 6, 1967.

KGW-TV aired an image similar to this one for television viewers to imagine Haystack Rock behind a fence. (Image created by Alix Smith)

Immediately after the Beach Bill became law, the Oregon Highway Commission began a survey of the entire coast to establish a permanent beach zone line, and the coordinates of that survey line became an integral part of the law. The line generally corresponds to the presence of vegetation backing the sand, and it remains today as the jurisdictional limit to define the state's easement for recreational use by the public.

The legislation was challenged by coastal developers and was reviewed by the courts over the next few years. The Oregon Supreme Court, in upholding the legislation, noted that "the dry-sand area in Oregon has been enjoyed by the general public as a recreational adjunct of the wet-sand or foreshore area since the beginning of the state's political history." And "from the time of the earliest settlement to the present day, the general public has assumed that the dry-sand area was a part of the public beach." In 1972, federal judges upheld the legality of the legislation.

As noted in various written accounts documenting the passage of the Beach Bill, a number of key players contributed to the successful resolution of this landmark legislation. As House Highway Committee chair, Bazett championed the bill and was instrumental in facilitating its passage. Although he was more of a behind-the-scenes player, then State Treasurer Bob Straub openly advocated for and testified on the bill's behalf. Effective

> Dear Governor McCall
>
> I vote not to have fences all over the beach, because it is a free country. People may start fights, or injure someone, we wouldn be able to have fun or have a nice picnic, and their will be complaints. So, I hope we don't let it happen,
>
> A future
>   voter
>   Dianny
>   Cobb
>   Sellwood School
>   Grade 4
>   Room 24

MAY 12 1967

This is just one of the many letters sent to Governor McCall in support of the Beach Bill. (Courtesy of Oregon State Archives)

media coverage certainly influenced the outcome by piquing the interest of the public. A number of citizen activists organized and continued, even after the passage of the bill, to be involved in protecting the beaches.

But for many Oregonians, the Beach Bill is primarily remembered as McCall's signature achievement and the basis for the legacy he envisioned. It is well worth making a field trip to the second floor of the State Capitol in Salem to view Governor McCall's life-sized portrait, painted by Henk Pander, which memorializes McCall's innate leadership in ensuring Oregon's beaches remain without fences.

DAY 4

Cannon Beach to Arch Cape

Distance: 7.3 miles

Terrain: Beach, road

Begin: Cannon Beach Library, 131 N Hemlock Street

Directions: Traveling north on US Highway 101, take the Cannon Beach City Center (Ecola State Park) exit between mileposts 29 and 30, travel west on Sunset Boulevard to Hemlock, turn right, and proceed 0.6 mile to the library.

Traveling south on US Highway 101, take the Cannon Beach City Center (Ecola State Park) exit at milepost 28, follow Fir Street (it changes to Elm Avenue and E 3rd Street), turn left on Spruce, right on 3rd Street, and left onto North Hemlock.

Parking is available in a public lot behind the library.

End: Arch Cape Creek Suspension Bridge

Directions: From US Highway 101, between mileposts 34 and 35, just north of the Arch Cape tunnel, turn east onto E Beach Road and left onto E Shingle Mill Lane. Follow it as it curves around through the east side of the Arch Cape community to 3rd Road. There is limited street parking in the neighborhood and an area for two to three cars at the trailhead.

General public transportation is available with Sunset Transportation Services between Cannon Beach and Manzanita, and it may be possible to prearrange for the driver to make a special stop in Arch Cape.

Overview

Today's hike begins by walking a bit through Cannon Beach, then proceeds along the excellent sand beach past Haystack Rock and over the same rock shelf used by early travelers to round Hug Point, and finally ends in Arch Cape.

This hike requires close consultation with the tide table because rounding Hug Point and passing other rock outcroppings, which are reached between miles 3 and 5, is only possible near low tide. Plus, tide pools at the base of Haystack Rock are exposed during low tide, and you might be interested in exploring them. Another highlight includes the opportunity to catch a glimpse of Oswald West's summer home.

Description

Begin at the Cannon Beach Library on N Hemlock Street. Walk south on Hemlock to 1st Avenue, turn right, and proceed straight ahead to access the beach. This is excellent sand for walking—as good as it gets. Turn south and head toward Haystack Rock, reached 1 mile into the hike. There, you can take a few moments to explore the living tide pools revealed at low tide.

Sadly, Oregon's sea star (another name for starfish, which isn't really a fish) population is being decimated by sea star wasting disease. This condition has occurred in other western states, but until the spring of 2014, it was not prevalent in Oregon waters. The disease is rapidly spreading among the sea star population, to the point that within a period of six months, over half were affected, and it could result in complete extinction of some species. Affected sea stars lose their limbs and can't hold on to rocks or piers; their bodies literally fall apart, and they disintegrate into mush.

Scientists recently determined that a virus, which has actually been present in the species for many years, is causing the syndrome. They are trying to determine how it has recently resulted in the largest marine disease outbreak ever recorded. Likewise, they are attempting to predict the impact that the complete loss of the sea star population would have on the entire marine intertidal ecosystem.

Day 4: Cannon Beach to Arch Cape

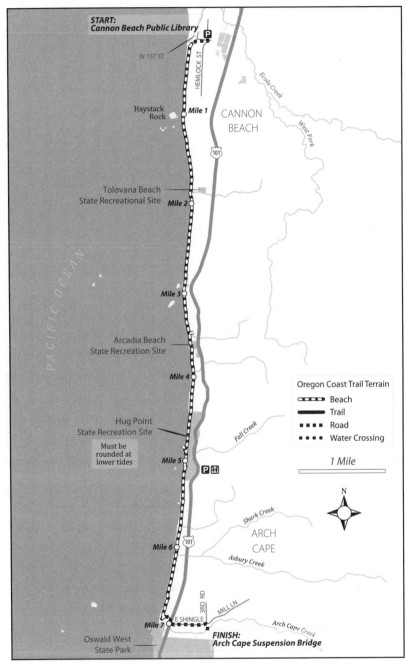

Early twentieth-century traveling by auto around Hug Point was an adventure. (Oregon Historical Society Research Library, bb012847)

Look up to notice the row of pleasant, brown-shingled cottages and houses perched on the bluff. On the far edge of the ridge to the south, just before a clump of trees, sits a light-colored log cabin in a modified Adirondack design. The original house on this site was built for Governor Oswald West in 1913 and served as his family's coastal retreat until he sold it in 1936. The home was destroyed by fire in 1991 and was then reconstructed in the original design. It is now privately owned and is listed on the National Register of Historic Places.

Continue south and walk around or through a couple of smaller rocky points until reaching Hug Point at 4.7 miles. It may be possible to get around Hug Point on the sand at very low tide, but more likely you will walk on a small rock shelf just above the water. This shelf is the remains of a primitive roadbed that was blasted out of the head around the turn of the twentieth century to facilitate travel to Arch Cape, which at the time was accessible only by driving a horse-drawn or motorized vehicle on the beach. Follow the ledge around the point and hop back down onto the beach; you might have to wade a short distance from the point to the shore, depending on the tide.

Continue walking 2 miles along the beach, past the houses of Arch Cape. Approaching the headland—almost but not all the way to it—look for a well-defined path off the sand and through a bed of rocks that leads to Leech Lane. Head east on this road until almost reaching the highway, which is in sight straight ahead, and turn right onto Cannon Road. Follow it as it turns east and passes under the highway onto E Shingle Mill Lane. Continue walking on this road about 0.25 mile to 3rd Road; turn right and end the hike at the Arch Cape Creek suspension bridge. Look for the Oregon Coast Trail markers on 3rd Road, as the bridge is not immediately visible from the street.

DAY 5

Arch Cape to Neahkahnie Mountain

Distance: 9.3 miles

Terrain: Trail

Begin: Arch Cape Creek Suspension Bridge

Directions: From US Highway 101, between mileposts 34 and 35, just north of the Arch Cape tunnel, turn east onto E Beach Road and left onto E Shingle Mill Lane. Follow it as it curves around through the east side of the Arch Cape community to 3rd Road. There is limited street parking in the neighborhood and an area for two to three cars at the trailhead.

End: Neahkahnie Mountain (north trailhead)

Directions: From US Highway 101, turn west between mileposts 40 and 41 (1.1 miles north of the Short Sand Parking Area) into the (unnamed) gravel wayside with a small parking area to access the trailhead, which is directly across the highway.

Overview

This hike is characterized by diverse terrain, ranging from deep old-growth forest to vistas with panoramic ocean views to open meadows abundant with wildflowers in the spring and summer. The trail begins with an ascent, and although there are occasional switchbacks or downhill stretches, much of the first part of the trail is a steady elevation gain. The trail takes you to points close to—and directly overlooking—Short Sand Beach, but no time is spent walking on sand. Some parts of the trail (particularly approaching Short Sand Beach) can be very muddy and slippery, and the many exposed tree roots present a hiking challenge.

There is a total elevation gain of 2,321 feet and a total elevation loss of 1,910 feet.

Description

Begin the hike at a marked trailhead located on the east side of 3rd Road, just beyond where it intersects with E Shingle Mill Lane in Arch Cape. The trail begins with a suspension footbridge over Arch Cape Creek. Follow it up a short distance and turn left at the post toward Cape Falcon. The trail climbs gradually through a forest with a lovely spongy trail bed and then descends to US Highway 101, meeting it at 1.4 miles. Walk south on the highway a short distance, taking care to avoid oncoming traffic, and cross when the trail is visible on the west side of the highway.

The next mile or so stays within view of the highway, through old-growth forest, and crosses Falcon Cove Road at about 2.8 miles. The trail heads west on a moderate grade and then begins to climb to a clearing with ocean views. From there, it descends and then begins a gradual undulation along the shoreline. At the trail junction at about 7.7 miles into the hike, turn right, following the sign to the beach and approaching the simple memorial plaque and bench dedicated to journalist Matt Kramer that overlooks Short Sand Beach. This is the kind of spot to sit and contemplate just about anything.

The trail picks up again at the picnic area, just to the right of the drinking fountain. Cross a bridge over Short Sand Creek, turn right at the next junction, and walk over the suspension bridge at Necarney Creek. At the next juncture, keep right and head up the hillside until, after about 1 mile, it levels out.

The last segment of the hike (Elk Flats Trail) passes through a meadow and emerges onto a grassy hillside. Continue up the short rise to the wayside, directly across the highway from the north side of the Neahkahnie Mountain trailhead.

Day 5: Arch Cape to Neahkahnie Mountain

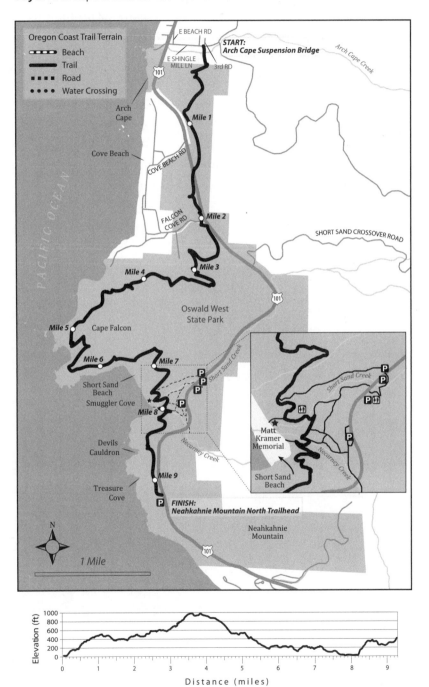

Matt Kramer was a journalist whose typewriter was an instrument of change for Oregon beaches. A reporter with the Associated Press, his beat included covering the 1967 Oregon legislative session. Kramer is widely credited for coining the term *Beach Bill*. His numerous articles about the pending legislation piqued the public's interest in the topic and generated widespread and grassroots support for its passage. After he died of cancer in 1972 at the age of fifty-four, the State of Oregon installed this memorial to honor his contribution to keeping all of Oregon's beaches open to the public.

DAY 6

Neahkahnie Mountain to Manzanita

Distance: 6.9 miles

Terrain: Trail, road, highway, beach

Begin: Neahkahnie Mountain (north trailhead)

Directions: From US Highway 101, turn west between mileposts 40 and 41 (1.1 miles north of the Short Sand Parking Area) into the (unnamed) gravel wayside with a small parking area to access the trailhead, which is directly across the highway.

End: Manzanita, at Laneda Avenue and Ocean Road

Directions: From US Highway 101, turn west between mileposts 43 and 44 at the Manzanita exit, which is Laneda Avenue. Drive to the end of Laneda and look for parking there or on any of the side streets.

Overview

This day's hike begins at the north end of the trail over Neahkahnie Mountain, climbs to a peak resplendent with panoramic views, and ends in the town of Manzanita. The trail, located within Oswald West State Park, is a popular day hike both for visitors and local residents. You should be attentive to the many switchbacks along the main trail; occasionally a spur trail is confusing and leads to nowhere.

Upon descending the mountain, a gravel road continues 0.3 mile to the highway, and you must walk 1.25 miles along the highway shoulder until reaching Nehalem Road, which leads to Neahkahnie Beach.

• •

Neahkahnie is one of many places along the coast with a name beginning with the Indian prefix *ne-*, which is related to villages or places.

• •

Description

Start at the parking area on the west side of US Highway 101 and carefully
cross it to find a brown cedar post located at the foot of the north trailhead
for Neahkahnie Mountain. You will be able to hear the highway for the
first 0.5 mile or so; the trail begins a steady climb, immediately providing
keyhole ocean views through the trees. It then transitions to a dense forest
setting occasionally dappled with sunlight and continually climbing uphill, sometimes in a steep ascent. After 2 miles, the trail will descend for a
while and then begin ascending again. At about 2.5 miles, you can either
climb up a steep hillside to the actual summit or continue walking along
the trail to begin heading down the other side of the mountain. Below,
the curved strand of beach, ocean waves, bay, and forest are laid out in a
coastal tapestry. Tattoo that onto your brain.

• •

The view from atop Neahkahnie Mountain is a fine reward for the
strenuous climb. It is a vista that has inspired many, including the
man who obtained it on our behalf, Samuel Boardman. About
Neahkahnie Mountain he wrote:

Neahkahnie Mountain rises directly above the sea at an elevation of 1,710 feet. While the ocean view is majestic, the rolling green timbered hills to the east are intensely inspiring. To the
west, the infinite space of conjecture as to what lies beyond the
horizon. The enigma of all who partake of life. To the east, the
material world that composes life itself. Where you have height
such as Neahkahnie, raise the people to it. Too much time of life
is spent in the valleys.

• •

Follow the path, a moderate downhill, through dense vegetation until it reaches a junction with a gravel road. Turn right and walk about 0.3
mile until you reach the highway, at 3.9 miles into the hike.

Day 6: Neahkahnie Mountain to Manzanita

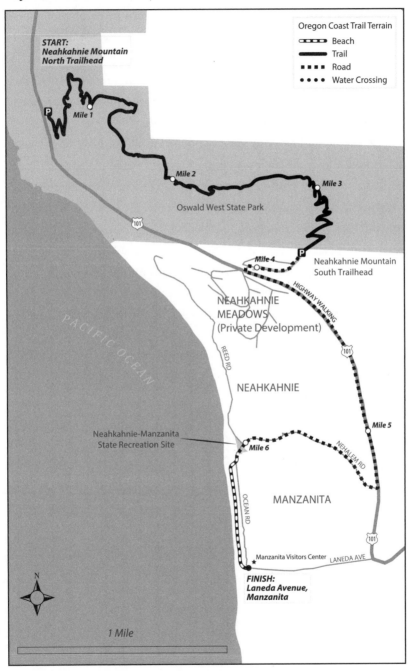

You will encounter the first significant gap in the Oregon Coast Trail at the base of Neahkahnie Mountain. Although private development does not often prevent access to the beach in Oregon, especially compared to other coastal states, such is the situation here, where 0.5 mile of roads located directly across the highway connecting the mountain to the beach are privately owned and maintained, and therefore cannot be incorporated into the OCT without the owners' permission.

Efforts are underway to identify opportunities for hikers that would avoid walking on the highway. Until then, this section is reluctantly included as the only public connection to the beach. When reaching US Highway 101, head south along the shoulder on the west side of the highway for 1.25 miles until reaching Nehalem Road. Turn west on Nehalem Road and walk 0.75 mile along the side of the road (there are no sidewalks) until returning to the beach, and continue walking south on the beach 0.5 mile to the foot of Laneda Avenue in Manzanita, where the hike ends. GPS coordinates for exiting the beach in Manzanita: N 45°43.111', W 123°56.480'.

DAY 7

Manzanita to Barview Jetty County Park (with boat ride) OR Manzanita to Nehalem Bay State Park (without boat ride)

Distance: 11 miles or 7 miles without boat ride

Terrain: Road, beach

Begin: Manzanita, at Laneda Avenue and Ocean Road

Directions: From US Highway 101, turn west between mileposts 43 and 44 at the Manzanita exit, which is Laneda Avenue. Drive to the end of Laneda and look for parking there or on any of the side streets.

End: Barview Jetty County Park

Directions: From US Highway 101, turn west between mileposts 53 and 54 at the sign for Barview Jetty County Park onto Cedar Street. Turn right on Trailer Park Road and jog left at Jetty Road. Follow it 0.6 mile to the end, where the South Jetty Parking Area is next to the lookout tower.

Without a boat ride, end at Nehalem Bay State Park. From US Highway 101, between mileposts 43 and 44, turn west and follow the signs to the park, reached after traveling 1.25 miles on local streets. Once inside the park, continue 1.7 miles to the beach-access day-use area. Parking and restrooms are available. Day-use fee or pass is required.

The Tillamook County Transportation District provides bus service between Manzanita and Rockaway Beach.

Overview

This hike combines walking local streets with long stretches of fantastic beaches and includes the first of three consecutive boat trips on the OCT.

If possible, time the hike so that a lower tide coincides with the boat trip across Nehalem Bay; otherwise, some highway walking is necessary. There is no significant elevation gain or loss on this hike.

Description

Option 1—Town walking: Begin the day at the foot of Laneda Avenue, Manzanita's main street. This route takes in Manzanita's back streets for the first mile or so and, in doing so, offers you glimpses of this charming town without adding any distance. Walk east on Laneda Avenue to Carmel Avenue and turn right. Just after Pacific Lane, the street divides. Follow Carmel to the left as it turns into a gravel path, ending at Sunset Lane, which has a well-established bike path on the east side of the street. Follow it past the pond and municipal golf course to where the street becomes Necarney Boulevard. Continue walking along the bike and pedestrian path until it ends at Glenesslin Lane, just past the entrance to Nehalem Bay State Park. Turn right on Glenesslin Lane and follow it back onto the beach.

Walk south 3 miles on the beach. As there are no houses along this stretch of the beach, which is adjacent to Nehalem Bay State Park, you are not likely to encounter many people except for the occasional runner, horseback rider, or dog walker.

Option 2—Beach walking: You can also head south from Laneda Avenue and continue walking along the beach for 4 miles.

••

The land that composes and is adjacent to Nehalem Bay State Park was once envisioned as a booming resort area and was therefore platted for development in 1908. But few people bought lots on Nehalem Spit, and many of those who did lost their property for failing to pay taxes during the Great Depression. After acquiring these properties in the 1930s, Tillamook County transferred the land in a series of gifts to the State of Oregon for a park, which opened in 1972.

••

At 0.1 mile before reaching the jetty, take the signed horse and hiking trail leading up off the beach and through the shallow dunes. Follow the

Day 7: Manzanita to Barview Jetty County Park

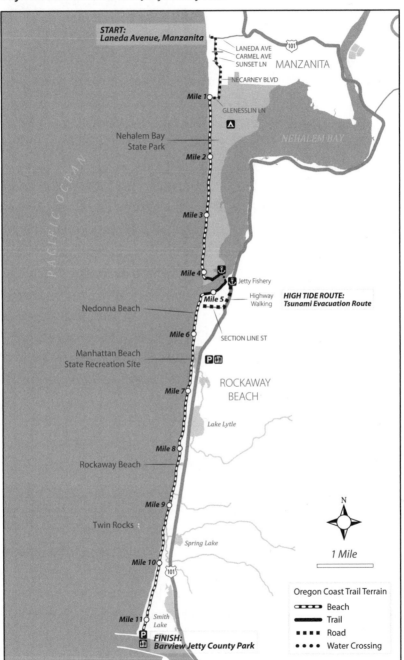

START:
Laneda Avenue, Manzanita

LANEDA AVE
CARMEL AVE
SUNSET LN

MANZANITA

NECARNEY BLVD

Mile 1

GLENESSLIN LN

Nehalem Bay
State Park

NEHALEM BAY

Mile 2

PACIFIC OCEAN

Mile 3

Mile 4

Jetty Fishery

Mile 5   Highway
               Walking

HIGH TIDE ROUTE:
Tsunami Evacuation Route

Nedonna Beach

Mile 6

SECTION LINE ST

Manhattan Beach
State Recreation Site

Mile 7

ROCKAWAY
BEACH

Lake Lytle

Mile 8

Rockaway Beach

Mile 9

Twin Rocks

Spring Lake

Mile 10

Mile 11   Smith
           Lake

FINISH:
Barview Jetty County Park

N

1 Mile

Oregon Coast Trail Terrain
▭▭▭▭ Beach
━━━━ Trail
▪ ▪ ▪ ▪ Road
● ● ● ● Water Crossing

sandy path until it intersects with another trail; take a right turn and head toward the water. Walk 0.5 mile through tall grasses and shrubbery to a small beach directly across Nehalem Bay from Jetty Fishery.

Arrangements can be made ahead of time with Jetty Fishery (see page 18 for contact information) to transport hikers across the bay for a fee, or you can call them once you have arrived at the beach. This same location has been used to ferry walkers for many years. In 1929, Guy and Barbara Reynolds described reaching the end of the spit: "It is about four miles down this flat hard beach to the river, and across the tip of the sand spit to the river bank opposite the railway station of Jetty, where a hail across the narrow stream will bring the fisherman who lives there, over to ferry you across." It is nice, indeed, that some traditions live on.

This is the easiest of the boat rides to arrange, as it is not necessary to make reservations ahead of time. It is highly recommended, therefore, to take a boat. If you prefer not to do this, you can take the same horse and hiking trail and, instead of heading toward the water, head north and walk 2 miles to the day-use area of Nehalem Bay State Park to end the hike there. (To resume the OCT from here, I recommend skipping over 12 miles of highway walking between Manzanita and Rockaway Beach and starting to hike again at the Nehalem Bay south jetty just north of Section Line Street in Rockaway Beach.)

After the short boat ride, you'll need to find your way back to the beach, and there are a couple of possibilities for continuing south. The first is to cross the picnic area to a path down to a marshland, which you can usually cross at lower tides, to access and walk on top of the old rock jetty for about 0.5 mile until reaching the beach. The jetty peters out for the last 0.1 mile or so, and you'll need to negotiate piles of driftwood and boulders to reach the beach.

If the tide does not allow access to the jetty by walking through the marsh, or if you prefer to avoid walking on the jetty, head the short distance east to US Highway 101. Turn right and walk along the west shoulder of the highway until, just before reaching 0.5 mile, a stairway leads down from the highway on the right. This stairway serves as the Tsunami Evacuation Route for the community of Rockaway; the first set of stairs ends at the railroad track. Cross the tracks and take the second set of stairs to the left. The stairs will deposit you on Section Line Street. Walk 0.3 mile on this street to the beach.

• •

Eventually, it is envisioned that the Salmonberry Corridor Trail will intersect with the Oregon Coast Trail at the south jetty and will head south along the railroad tracks all the way to Tillamook. The Salmonberry Corridor project would convert a currently un-used 86-mile rail corridor to recreational use by connecting the existing Banks–Vernonia rail trail with Tillamook via a combina-tion of paved and natural surface paths. Funding has not yet been secured for constructing the trail, and it could take years, if not decades, for the trail to be fully realized.

• •

Continue south for 6 miles along Nedonna, Manhattan, and Rockaway Beaches to the jetty. Turn left into the parking area of Barview Jetty County Park, where this hike ends.

DAY 8

Garibaldi Marina to Netarts Landing (with boat ride) OR Cape Meares to Netarts Landing (without boat ride)

Distance: 12 miles with boat ride, 8 miles without boat ride

Terrain: Trail, beach, trail; boat ride recommended

Begin: Garibaldi Marina if taking a boat

Cape Meares (Bayocean Road and 4th Street) without boat

Directions: If taking a boat from Garibaldi Marina: From US Highway 101 (referred to in Garibaldi as Garibaldi Avenue), turn west between mileposts 55 and 56 and follow signs to the Port of Garibaldi by turning west on S 7th Street. Follow it to the marina, where there is parking.

Without a boat ride, beginning at Cape Meares: From US Highway 101 in Tillamook, between mileposts 65 and 66, turn west onto 3rd Street, which will turn into Oregon Highway 131. Take it 1.8 miles and then turn right onto Bayocean Road NW. Follow it 6 miles (it will change names to 13th Street NW and Meares Avenue NW) until it ends, at 4th Street NW in Cape Meares, where there is parking for a few cars.

End: Netarts Landing County Boat Launch

Directions: From US Highway 101 in Tillamook, turn west onto 3rd Street, between mileposts 65 and 66, which becomes Oregon Highway 131. Continue 5 miles to Netarts and turn left onto Netarts Bay Drive. Follow it to Netarts Landing, where there is parking for a fee.

Public transportation is available with the Tillamook County Transportation District between Garibaldi and Tillamook, and between Tillamook and Netarts (transfer required).

Overview

This guide recommends eliminating two difficult miles of walking along US Highway 101 between Barview Jetty County Park and Garibaldi, which provides little, if any, shoulder suitable for pedestrians. For that reason, this day's hike starts in a different place than the previous day's hike ends. Long-term (but as yet unfunded) plans are to develop a pedestrian path here adjacent to the railroad tracks as part of the future Salmonberry Corridor Trail.

This day has a little of everything, so what's not to like? You'll start with a boat ride across Tillamook Bay, and then walk the length of Bayocean Spit, which is home to an interesting chapter of Oregon coastal history and also an excellent location for bird watching. The hike then continues up and over scenic Cape Meares to a lighthouse and the iconic Octopus Tree, and it ends by walking through the picturesque communities of Oceanside and Netarts.

Description

Option 1—Boat Ride: You are encouraged to arrange a boat ride across Tillamook Bay by contacting Garibaldi Marina the day before transportation is needed (see page 18 for contact information). They will confirm the exact time of departure, depending on tides and schedule. The hike for this option totals 12 miles, as it includes 4 miles along Bayocean Spit.

Option 2—No Boat Ride: If you do not take a boat, you should skip 18 miles of highway walking and begin the hike in the small community of Cape Meares, where you can access the beach at a small parking area at the foot of Bayocean Road. This would eliminate the first 4 miles of walking down the spit, but the rest of the hike is the same as for Option 1.

If you take a boat, you'll be dropped off at Crab Harbor, where the trail (actually an old road) runs right along the bay shore. Begin by walking south down the trail and cut over to the ocean beach to the west either at the gate where the trail leaves the forest (3 miles from the north end of the spit) or at the trailhead (1 mile farther). Resume walking on the beach to the community of Cape Meares. The alternate hike, if a boat is not taken, would begin here.

Day 8: Garibaldi to Netarts Landing

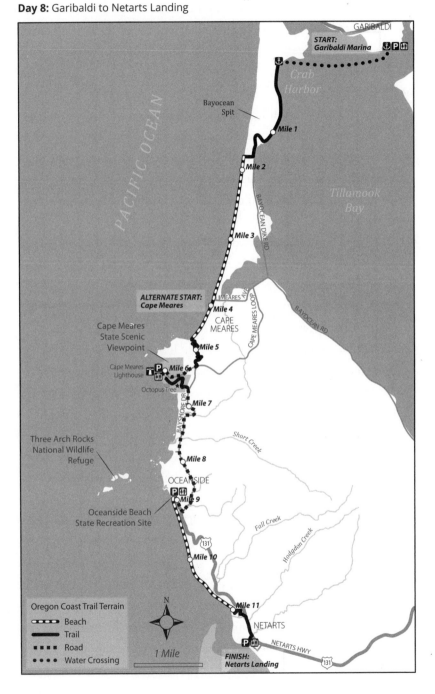

Once you reach Cape Meares, after about 0.5 mile down the beach, the sand gives way to rocks and boulders with very little or no beach during high tide. Scramble along the rocks and beach until staring into the face of the cliff and you can go no farther. Look for an egress off the beach leading up a short but steep path that is conveniently equipped with a rope; haul yourself up the short slippery slope. Walk a mile uphill to the top of the cape (bearing right at a junction after about 0.25 mile). The trail is nicely accommodating to the feet and travels through old-growth forest with occasional dramatic views to the north. Upon reaching a juncture, turn right onto the road leading to the Cape Meares State Scenic Viewpoint.

The viewpoint offers a network of trails leading to scenic outlets, an information center, the Cape Meares Lighthouse, and the Octopus Tree—all worth exploring.

. . . .

At thirty-eight feet high, the Cape Meares Lighthouse is the shortest lighthouse on the Oregon Coast, but its lantern room holds the large first-order French Fresnel lens. The Friends of Cape Meares helped save the lighthouse some years ago from being torn down, as it had been vandalized on several occasions. In 2010, several rounds of ammunition were fired at the lantern room, breaking fifteen panes of glass and several prisms in the Fresnel lens. The cost to repair the damages was $500,000; the vandals were arrested and pleaded guilty to the crime. The lighthouse is now owned by the US Coast Guard and managed by OPRD. Cape Meares Lighthouse can be toured daily April through October.

. . . .

In resuming the hike, take the path to the Octopus Tree, skirt to the right of it, and continue 0.75 mile on a wooded path to Cape Meares Loop (which is part of the Scenic Capes Highway). Turn right and follow it south 2 miles to the community of Oceanside. Although referred to as a highway, the road is not difficult to walk, but it is best to cross the road several times to find the widest shoulder as it narrows or disappears altogether in places.

The Octopus Tree at Cape Meares is a designated Oregon Heritage Tree. (Photo by Bob Reed, Friends of Cape Meares Lighthouse)

The Octopus Tree measures more than fourteen feet across at its base and has no central trunk. Limbs extend horizontally as much as thirty feet before turning upward. The tree is 105 feet tall and is estimated to be around two hundred fifty years old. Its unique shape could result from an oddity of nature, or Native Americans may have deliberately shaped it to hold cedar canoes and other ritual objects for a ceremonial burial site.

Entering Oceanside, turn right and follow the sign to the Oceanside Beach State Recreation Site. From there, walk south along the beach for about 3 miles, glancing behind you as you leave Oceanside to admire the pretty town perched on the hillside.

If there is less hard sand to walk on at higher tides, look for a way off the beach and walk the last few blocks on the street to reach Netarts Landing, where the hike ends.

Bayocean Park

If you arrange a boat ride from Garibaldi to Bayocean Spit, you will be dropped off at a small cove on the bay side of the spit. Although there is no evidence of it now, this place owns a remarkable place in Oregon history.

In 1906, a wealthy real estate promoter from Kansas City named T. B. Potter visited Oregon and, together with his son, envisioned an ambitious coastal resort on Bayocean Spit. He platted Bayocean and sold two thousand lots. Some new residents stayed temporarily in Tent City (later named Bungalow City) until their houses were built. Potter also built a hotel and a natatorium for indoor swimming, complete with saltwater and waves generated with a surf machine. Despite ongoing problems with developing infrastructure, such as telephones, electricity, and roads, a post office was established in 1909, and by 1912 the community was flourishing. The population in 1914 totaled two thousand.

Early visitors arrived via steamship, a trip that took three days from Portland and involved a difficult passage, resulting in local homeowners requesting that the US Army Corps of Engineers build a jetty. The Corps of Engineers recommended that two jetties be built and required that local contributions cover half the cost (the total cost for two jetties was estimated at $2.2 million). To save costs, the local community agreed only to the development of one jetty, which was completed in 1917. The provision of the jetty did make for smoother sailing, though by then people had started to arrive by train, a much faster journey.

Within a few years, the beach on Bayocean Spit began to narrow and erode significantly. In 1932, a major storm destroyed the natatorium,

No 284 BUNGALOW CITY BAY OCEAN, ORE.

Families with small children often stayed at Bungalow City. (Oregon Historical Society Research Library, bb012844)

and over the next few years, other structures, including the hotel, began to give way to the elements. In 1952, another storm breached the entire spit, causing the destruction of valuable oyster beds. A second jetty was finally built in 1973, which stabilized the beaches, but by then the town had been abandoned. Today there are no remains at all of this community, although the schoolhouse was moved to Cape Meares, where it is now used as a community center.

DAY 9

Netarts Landing to Sand Lake Recreation Area

Distance: 13 miles

Terrain: Beach, trail; boat ride optional

Begin: Netarts Landing County Boat Launch

Directions: From US Highway 101 in Tillamook, turn west between mileposts 65 and 66 onto 3rd Street, which becomes Oregon Highway 131. Continue 5 miles to Netarts and turn left onto Netarts Bay Drive. Follow it to Netarts Landing, where there is parking for a fee.

End: Sand Lake Recreation Area, West Winds Day-Use Area

Directions: From US Highway 101, turn west between mileposts 76 and 77 onto Sandlake Road. Follow it 4 miles and turn left at the intersection with Cape Lookout Road (staying on Sandlake Road). After a mile, turn right onto Galloway Road and follow it to the end to the West Winds Day-Use Area parking lot. Daily recreation fee, applicable federal recreation pass, or Oregon Pacific Coast Passport required.

Overview

Ideally, begin this hike with the last of three boat rides on consecutive days, this time from Netarts Landing to the tip of Netarts Spit. While there is not a designated boat provider, you may be able to hitch a ride from someone willing to take you to the spit from the landing. If you do arrange a boat ride, begin this hike where you are dropped off, at the north end of Netarts Spit. The walk continues along the ocean side of the spit into

Cape Lookout State Park and ends with another stretch of satisfying beach walking. The last part, however, may be shared with off-highway vehicles.

If you don't take a boat ride, the alternative is not unpleasant, as you can walk the 5 miles from Netarts Landing into Cape Lookout State Park. Or, to shorten the hike and avoid road walking altogether, you can just begin the hike at Cape Lookout State Park.

Description

Option 1—Boat Ride: If you can arrange it, take a boat from Netarts Landing to Netarts Spit, and hike down the spit about 5 miles to the picnic and day-use area at Cape Lookout State Park, recognizable from the beach by a round gazebo-like structure. This is the longest spit on the coast and, especially at the north end, can be quite secluded. You should walk along the ocean side of the spit, as marshes and wetlands can impede or make passage impossible on the bay side.

While this hike is not strictly tide dependent, the beach just north of the park narrows during high tide. If it becomes too difficult to walk on the beach, about 0.5 mile before reaching the park area, cut across the beach to the campground at designated access points. Walk through the main campground and the group campground areas, and pick up a trail that leads to the gazebo. About 100 yards farther south is a driftwood memorial to Dick Winsor, longtime manager of Cape Lookout State Park. The sign indicating the North Trail is next to the memorial.

Option 2—No Boat Ride: If you do not take a boat ride, walk the 5 miles to Cape Lookout State Park by heading south on Netarts Bay Road, which is also at times referred to as Whiskey Creek Road. This is a scenic and pastoral road next to the bay, but it does not always provide a generous shoulder for walking. For the most part, the grade is moderate with a few undulating stretches. After 5 miles, turn onto Cape Lookout Road, and it's another 0.8 mile to the day-use area to find access to the North Trail.

Or, to eliminate road walking altogether, begin the hike in the day-use area of Cape Lookout State Park. After this point, the routing options are the same.

Day 9: Netarts Landing to Sand Lake Recreation Area

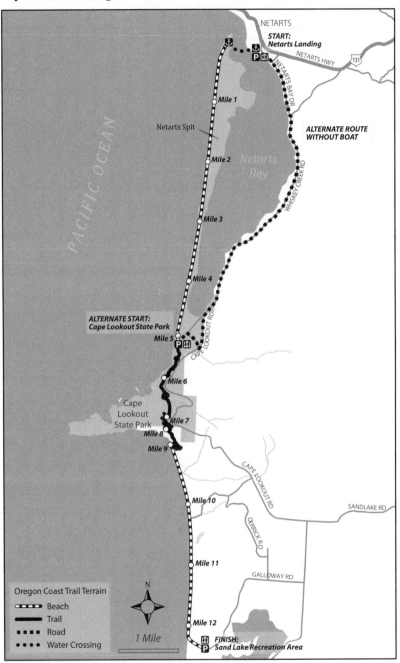

However you get to Cape Lookout State Park, take the North Trail, which begins a short distance south of the day-use area on a path next to an information sign and map, for 2.3 miles to the top of the cape. It winds up and up through the woods. After 1.2 miles, pass a spur road leading out to Cape Lookout Road. Stick to the main trail, crossing Cape Creek on an impressive cable suspension bridge shortly thereafter. The trail continues along a rolling grade to emerge at the top of the cape. From there, take the path heading out to the tip of the cape, but at the first junction, reached in less than 0.1 mile, make a sharp left turn down the hill toward the beach. From here, the South Trail descends at a moderate grade, back and forth, for 1.8 miles through a lovely forest, ending on the beach at the foot of the cape.

Continue down the beach a total of 3.75 miles to the Sand Lake Recreation Area West Winds Day-Use Area. The recreational area is part of the Siuslaw National Forest, and for the last 2 miles or so, the beach is shared with off-highway vehicles (OHVs). Look for a small dune leading to the parking area, where there's a sign indicating the boundary for vehicle use.

Although fortunately not a frequent occurrence, various recreational activities on the beaches at times conflict with each other. Motor vehicles are allowed on some beaches, and hikers have to share space with them. The same is true of OHVs, which are likely to be present near Sand Lake and in parts of the Oregon Dunes National Recreation Area. Thus, walking along the beaches is not always the pristine or quiet experience many are expecting.

DAY 10

Sand Lake Recreation Area to Pacific City

Distance: 11 miles without fording lake, 5 miles with fording lake
Terrain: Beach, road
Begin: Sand Lake Recreation Area, West Winds Day-Use Area
Directions: From US Highway 101, between mileposts 76 and 77, turn west onto Sandlake Road. Follow it 4 miles and turn left at the intersection with Cape Lookout Road (staying on Sandlake Road). After a mile, turn right onto Galloway Road, and follow it to the end to the West Winds Day-Use Area parking lot. Daily recreation fee, applicable federal recreation pass, or Oregon Pacific Coast Passport required.
End: Pacific City, corner of Pacific Avenue and Sunset Drive
Directions: From US Highway 101, turn west between mileposts 90 and 91 onto Brooten Road. Follow it 3 miles to Pacific Avenue. Turn left, drive over the small bridge, and look for parking at a small parking area next to the beach; some limited street parking is also available.

Overview

The outcome of today's hike depends on the tides and your willingness to attempt fording Sand Lake. At very low tide in the summer, you can allegedly ford the lake to avoid over 6 miles of road walking. If you don't cross it, you can take local roads to the beach again at Tierra del Mar. A highlight is crossing over Cape Kiwanda.

Here is the outlet of Sand Lake at low tide. It's difficult to gauge the lake's depth even when standing next to it.

Description

Option 1—Local Roads: I recommend circumventing Sand Lake by walking along local roads until accessing the beach again in Tierra del Mar. For the most part, walking the local roads is not an unpleasant alternative. The roads are scenic, and no walking is required along US Highway 101. This option is about 6 miles longer than that of crossing Sand Lake.

Begin by heading east from the parking area at West Winds Day-Use Area on Galloway Road, the main road heading out of Sand Lake Recreational Area. For the first 0.5 mile or so, the road goes through the recreation site, and then it transitions into a picturesque country lane adjacent to bucolic fields that are home to black-and-white cows. Walk up Galloway Road 2.5 miles until it intersects with Three Capes Highway (Sandlake Road).

Turn right (south) and walk 4 miles along Sandlake Road, passing a few houses, fields, and dilapidated barns. Continue through this lovely pastoral setting on the west side of the road, which has a well-established bike trail for much of the way. The road is mainly level, with a few ups and downs. While walking Sandlake Road is less hectic by far than walking along the highway, it is not always pleasant walking along the shoulder. If

Day 10: Sand Lake Recreation Area to Pacific City

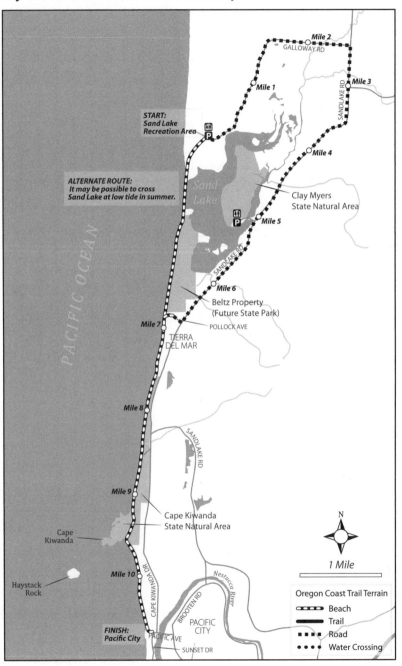

you are willing to detour 0.5 mile or so, restrooms, water, and picnic areas are available at Whalen Island (Clay Myers State Natural Area), reached at about 4.5 miles into the hike.

Option 2—Cross Sand Lake: One option, at low tide and during the summer months, is to wade across Sand Lake. Even under the best of conditions, however, crossing the lake can be difficult because it is wide and may be deep at times. The tide changes very rapidly, and it doesn't provide for secure footing. Based on my own observation (I have not personally tried it) and on experiences reported by others, attempting the crossing can be a harrowing experience; nonetheless, some insist it can be done.

The outlet to Sand Lake is 0.75 mile south of West Winds Day-Use Area; if you cross it, merely resume walking on the beach all the way to Pacific City.

••

In late 2014, OPRD acquired 357 acres of coastal property in Tillamook County. Known as the Beltz Property, the plot sits along Sandlake Road north of Pacific City and south of Cape Lookout State Park, and will be developed into a new park with trails to provide access to the beach closer than Tierra del Mar.

••

Once in Tierra del Mar, turn west on Pollock Avenue (the second road you come to) at the north end of the small community and follow it until it dead-ends. Take a short sandy pathway through the grasses leading to the beach.

Walk 3.7 miles on the beach and over Cape Kiwanda, which is really one big sand dune. Once descending from the cape, you'll be in Pacific City. Walk another mile on the beach and exit over a small foredune between two sandy clumps of vegetation onto Pacific Avenue. The intersection of Pacific Avenue and Sunset Drive is about a block east, next to the sign indicating Bob Straub State Park. GPS coordinates for exiting the beach in Pacific City: N 45°12.128', W 123°58.091'

DAYS 11–20

Pacific City to Florence

Overview

The next series of hikes begins in Pacific City at Bob Straub State Park, which is not officially part of the OCT because there is no egress from Nestucca Spit. It is the only out-and-back hike included in this guide. After learning about Bob Straub's leadership in preventing Nestucca Spit from becoming part of the highway, you will understand why the park came to be named for him and why it is included in this guide.

Day 12 takes you into the town of Neskowin; unfortunately, this short beach walk is sandwiched between stretches of highway where there is no trail. Beach walking resumes on Day 13 at the north end of Lincoln City (Roads End) to Schooner Creek. On Day 14, the trail begins in Gleneden on the beach, enters Fogarty Creek State Recreation Area, traverses a path adjacent to the highway through Boiler Bay State Scenic Viewpoint, and continues into Depoe Bay. For most of this stretch, the scenery is particularly dramatic and scenic because the shoreline is high and rocky with no beach. You can visit the Whale Watching Center in Depoe Bay along this hike as well, but check days and hours of operation in advance, as it is regularly closed two days a week.

Day 15 offers a long and satisfying beach walk between Devils Punchbowl and Yaquina Bay State Recreation Site. Day 16 begins where the previous day ends and takes you over (and under) the iconic Yaquina Bay Bridge, concluding with excellent beach walking. You will, on Day 17, begin at Seal Rock and continue all the way, mostly on sand, to Yachats, crossing the Alsea Bay Bridge.

Day 19 includes an easy stroll along the historic 804 Trail through the lovely town of Yachats and then includes a steep climb up Cape Perpetua along Amanda's Trail, which was named for a member of the Coos Indian tribe who was forcibly marched to an internment camp in the Yachats area in the mid-1850s. The last two days in this section are short but lovely walks along the beach and also include a visit to Heceta Head. The hikes in this section conclude at the north end of Florence.

I recommend skipping significant stretches of highway walking during this section, including between Pacific City and Winema Road, Neskowin and Roads End, and a section just south of Cape Perpetua. Altogether, 23 miles are eliminated. As a result, some of the hikes are shorter.

You will visit Neskowin, Lincoln City, Gleneden, Depoe Bay, Newport, Waldport, and Yachats, which all offer numerous places to stay and to enjoy a meal or two.

Table 4. Days 11–20: Pacific City to Florence

Day	Hike	Miles	Terrain	Considerations
11	Bob Straub State Park	4.5	Beach	out and back
12	Winema Road to Neskowin Beach SRS	5.5	Beach	
13	Roads End SRS to Schooner Creek	6.2	Beach, road	
14	Gleneden Beach SRS to Devils Punchbowl SNA	12.5	Beach, road, trail	
15	Devils Punchbowl SNA to Yaquina Bay SRS	9.8	Beach, road, highway	
16	Yaquina Bay SRS to Seal Rock SRS	10.5	Road, trail, beach	
17	Seal Rock SRS to Smelt Sands SRS	14.1 or 13.1**	Beach, road, trail	low tide

Day	Hike	Miles	Terrain	Considerations
18	Smelt Sands SRS to Cummins Creek Trailhead	8.6	Trail, road, highway	
19	Ocean Beach Picnic Area or Muriel O. Ponsler Memorial SSV to Heceta Head Lighthouse SSV	5.7 or 4.4**	Beach, trail	low tide
20	Baker Beach Campground to Siuslaw River North Jetty	5.5	Beach	

** Hike distance is based on tidal considerations.

Days 11–20: North Central Coast Overview

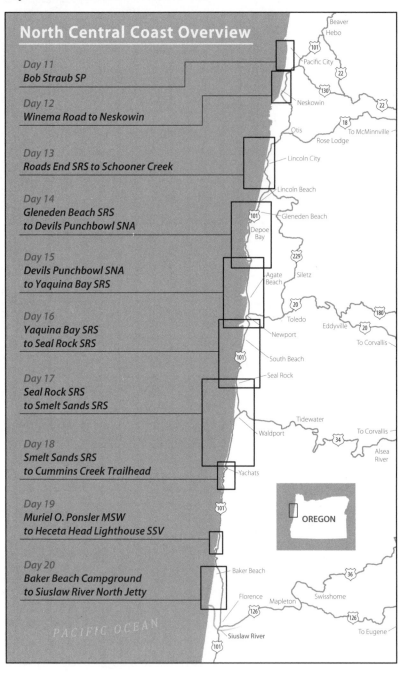

DAY 11

Bob Straub State Park

Distance: 4.5 miles

Terrain: Beach

Begin and End: Bob Straub State Park

Directions: From US Highway 101, turn west between mileposts 90 and 91 onto Brooten Road. Follow it 3 miles to Pacific Avenue. Turn left, drive over the small bridge, turn left onto Sunset Drive and left again to follow signs to the park, where there is ample parking.

Overview

This walk along Nestucca Spit in Bob Straub State Park is the only out-and-back hike suggested for this guide because, without a boat ride, there is no egress off the spit to continue south. As such, it deviates from the official Oregon Coast Trail, which bypasses it altogether, but it should not be missed, if for no other reason than to appreciate it is there at all.

Description

The hike itself is very straightforward. From the parking area, take the trail west across the dunes to the beach and head south. The tip of the spit is a 2.1-mile walk from the parking area. Round the tip to see Nestucca Bay, where harbor seals often bask in the sun. Retrace your steps to the parking area for a fine 4.5-mile beach walk.

Saving Nestucca Spit

As you stand at the quiet intersection of Pacific Avenue and Sunset Drive in Pacific City, imagine if instead you were in the middle of a four-lane highway—a nightmare scenario that came very close to becoming reality. US Highway 101, for the most part, runs close to the shoreline, but just north of Neskowin, it diverts some six miles inland, bypassing Tierra del Mar, Cape Kiwanda, and Pacific City and traveling instead through Beaver, Hebo, and Cloverdale. In 1965, the Oregon State Highway Commission approved a plan to "straighten" the highway so that it could more conveniently take people by car into the coastal communities. The plan was to move the highway so it would pass through Sand Lake and Cape Kiwanda, over the headland onto Nestucca Spit, and finally onto Winema Road.

Reactions to the plan were mixed. Some residents and vacation home owners were not supportive because of the impending destruction of the beaches and other scenic areas. On the other hand, some elected officials and many businesses supported the idea, believing it would encourage economic growth for the area by bringing people to the coast more directly.

The issue first came to the attention of then State Treasurer Bob Straub in February 1966. He met with local citizens concerned about the plan and visited the area himself. He quickly realized that the project had moved beyond the planning phase when he discovered engineering stakes already pounded into the sand. Straub aligned himself with a citizen activist group (Citizens to Save our Sands, or SOS) that organized around this issue to prevent the project. SOS provided testimony, wrote letters,

This aerial view of Nestucca Spit makes us appreciate that it did not become part of the highway. (Photo courtesy of OPRD)

and on Mother's Day 1966, sponsored a beach march to publicize their cause. Shortly thereafter, the Highway Commission announced it was "reconsidering" its decision.

The timing coincided with the November 1966 election, when a new governor—either Bob Straub or Tom McCall—would be elected. According to several accounts, Tom McCall promised the powerful and influential chair of the Highway Commission, Glenn Jackson, his support for the Nestucca Spit project in return for Jackson's endorsement in the Republican

Like Governors West and McCall before him, Straub and his family held a strong affinity for the Oregon Coast. Here, in a photo dating from 1966, they picnic next to Proposal Rock in Neskowin. (Photo courtesy of Western Oregon University Archives, Robert W. Straub Collection)

primary for governor. McCall was reelected, and on July 6, 1967, he signed the Beach Bill to provide public access to Oregon's beaches. The next day the Highway Commission reopened the Nestucca Spit issue.

Straub learned that portions of the land intended for the highway project had been given to the State of Oregon by the federal Bureau of Land Management (BLM) on the condition they be used for recreational purposes. Accompanied by Oregon Senator Wayne Morse, Straub decided to meet with the federal secretary of the interior to convince him to disapprove the application for construction. Fortunately for Oregonians, the secretary of the interior, Stewart Udall, took his role as steward of the land seriously (compared to the likes of, say, James Watt). Under Udall's tenure, the National Trails System Act was enacted, which resulted in the development of the Pacific Crest Trail and provided funding for the Appalachian Trail. Udall himself was an avid hiker and outdoor enthusiast, but surely he had little to gain by getting involved in a highway project in Oregon. He denied the highway project on the basis that the environmental impact of paving over a beach was more significant than the fiscal costs in developing an alternative approach. In a letter to Governor McCall he stated:

This editorial cartoon regarding the Udall decision was published in the *Oregonian* on August 29, 1967. (©1967, Oregonian Publishing Co. Reprinted with permission)

"If the new route costs a little more, so what? In our time a wise resource use demands that we always search for the best solution for the long run—and never simply settle for the cheapest solution."

McCall apparently learned of Udall's decision through a press release and, though most likely unhappy at not being informed directly, may have been relieved by the outcome since many considered his position on Nestucca Spit to be politically motivated and ill conceived. Shortly thereafter, Jackson, not used to losing battles, developed yet another highway plan that circumvented federal lands. Once again, citizen activists organized their opposition by collecting signatures, holding rallies, and speaking at public hearings. In December 1967 McCall withdrew his support for the project, and in 1968 it was finally abandoned.

In 1987, Governor Neil Goldschmidt dedicated Nestucca Spit as Bob Straub State Park.

DAY 12

Winema Road to Neskowin Beach State Recreation Site

Distance: 5.5 miles

Terrain: Beach

Begin: Winema Road

Directions: Turn west off US Highway 101 between mileposts 93 and 94 onto Winema Road and follow the paved road to the end, where parking for a few cars is available.

End: Neskowin Beach State Recreation Site

Directions: From US Highway 101, turn west between mileposts 97 and 98 into Neskowin Beach State Recreation Site. Ample public parking is available.

This guide suggests skipping 6 miles along local roads and US Highway 101 between Pacific City and Winema Road, and that you begin the hike at the foot of Winema Road.

Overview

This short beach walk picks up on the south side of the spit and ends in Neskowin Village.

Description

Heading south from the Nestucca River, the next place to access the beach is at the foot of Winema Road, where there is limited parking across from a private church camp. Begin here by turning right to walk north on the beach until it ends at Porter Point at the Nestucca River, in 1 mile. This portion of the beach is quiet, serene, and lovely enough

Foliage was used as early riprap in Neskowin, 1938. (Oregon Historical Society Research Library, bb012845)

Rock riprap now armors the shoreline in Neskowin, 2013.

to deviate slightly from the official trail by heading north and retracing steps back south.

Return and walk south about 4 miles until reaching Proposal Rock at Neskowin, where Neskowin Creek joins the ocean. Proposal Rock is actually a small island covered with wind-blown trees and other vegetation, and it may be difficult, especially on a foggy or misty day, to recognize it from a distance because it blends in with mountains in the background.

• •

Proposal Rock was named by a local resident whose daughter received a marriage proposal there. The original Indian name was *Schlock*.

• •

At Proposal Rock turn inland and follow the creek to the parking area.

The beach at Neskowin is disappearing. For many years the shoreline has been almost entirely supported with riprap to protect oceanfront properties. Riprap is rock or other materials used to armor shorelines to protect them from erosion. However, the presence of riprap prevents the movement and natural distribution of sand, which can result in a significant loss of beaches and may also worsen erosion to neighboring properties. In a ten-year span between 1998 and 2008, the beach at Neskowin retreated as much as 164 feet. During the winter, waves can reach—or breach—the riprap during storms or high tides.

DAY 13

Roads End State Recreation Site
to Schooner Creek

Distance: 6.2 miles

Terrain: Beach, road

Begin: Roads End State Recreation Site

Directions: From US Highway 101, between mileposts 112 and 113, turn northwest at the traffic light (adjacent to a major shopping center) onto Logan Road, and drive 0.9 mile to the Roads End State Recreation Site parking area.

End: Schooner Creek

Directions: From US Highway 101, between mileposts 118 and 119, turn west at a small wayside directly off the highway, where limited parking is available. Parking is also available nearby along SW 51st Street.

Public transportation is available via Lincoln County Transit near the starting and ending points of this hike.

Overview

One of the most significant gaps in the OCT is located between Neskowin and the north end of Lincoln City. At present, walkers are required to walk on highway shoulder with the exception of about 4.5 miles of trail (Forest Service Road 1861, which connects with Cascade Head Trail) sandwiched between unpleasant sections of highway walking. Therefore, I reluctantly (because it is a shame to miss hiking near or on Cascade Head) recommend this stretch be eliminated, and that you resume the OCT again at Roads End State Recreation Site. Fortunately, local trail advocates and agency personnel are developing new trails that will soon eliminate some of this gap.

This hike combines a long beach walk with a stroll through the historic area of Lincoln City.

··

Lincoln City was incorporated on March 3, 1965, uniting the cities of Delake, Oceanlake, and Taft and the unincorporated communities of Cutler City and Nelscott. But choosing a name for the new city proved controversial. A contest allowed residents and schoolchildren to propose names. The top five submissions were published as a ballot in the newspaper, including Miracle Beach, Lincoln City, Miracle City, Surfland, and Holiday Beach. The two most popular were Lincoln City and Surfland. Although Surfland was the name preferred by schoolchildren (and no wonder!), Lincoln City was chosen.

··

Description

Get on the beach at Roads End State Recreation Site and continue south along the beach for just under 6 miles, past Lincoln City, where there are many opportunities to detour for a meal. For the last mile or so, approaching Siletz Bay, you may prefer to get off the shoreline to find a well-established footpath at the base of the cliff because during high tide, the narrow strip of sloped beach makes for difficult walking.

If so, follow the footpath until it terminates at a small plaza and brick roundabout. Keep right and follow the sidewalk through the Lincoln City Old Town, which was previously known as Taft (named for President William Howard Taft). At the end of the road, which is SW 51st Street, turn right onto the highway shoulder. Walk as far as there is sidewalk, which ends at a small wayside where Schooner Creek meets the Pacific Ocean at Siletz Bay. This wayside offers a view of the creek and estuary from the south. The historical marker also tells the story of the great earthquake and tsunami that struck on January 26, 1700, destroying Native American villages all along the Pacific Northwest coast.

DAY 14

Gleneden Beach State Recreation Site to Devils Punchbowl State Natural Area

Distance: 12.5 miles

Terrain: Beach, road, trail

Begin: Gleneden Beach State Recreation Site

Directions: From US Highway 101, turn west at the sign to Gleneden Beach, between mileposts 122 and 123. Drive 0.2 mile on Wesler Street to Gleneden Beach State Recreation Site. Ample public parking is available here.

End: Devils Punchbowl State Natural Area

Directions: From US Highway 101 South, turn west on Otter Crest Loop, between mileposts 132 and 133, and follow signs to Devils Punchbowl.

From US Highway 101 North, turn west between mileposts 129 and 130 and follow Otter Crest Loop to 1st Street; turn left and follow it to the parking area on the right.

This guide recommends skipping 3.5 miles of walking the shoulder of US Highway 101 between Schooner Creek and Gleneden Beach State Recreation Site. While some of this stretch provides adequate passage for walkers, especially over water crossings, most of it provides little shoulder for walking.

Overview

Today's walk begins on Gleneden Beach and transitions to trail and road walking because high cliffs and rocky terrain prevent access to the beach, or there is no beach at all. This landscape provides for spectacular and dramatic views, especially at Boiler Bay State Scenic Viewpoint, through Depoe Bay, and along Otter Crest Loop. The Whale Watching Center in Depoe Bay is also a good place to learn about whales and to watch for them when they're migrating. Or it may be possible to catch a glimpse of two resident whales, O'Valentine and Scarback, who prefer to summer in Depoe Bay rather than migrating all the way to Alaska. It also incorporates a short but wonderful detour in Depoe Bay, the North Point Pedestrian Loop.

This hike is one of the longest in the book, but you can shorten it in a couple of ways. Beginning at Fogarty Creek State Recreation Area rather than Gleneden Beach State Recreation Site would eliminate about 3 miles, or ending at Cape Foulweather Lookout Observatory along Otter Crest Loop instead of Devils Punchbowl State Natural Area would shorten the walk by about 2 miles. Parking is available at both of these locations.

Description

Begin the hike by taking the paved path heading north from the parking area of Gleneden Beach State Recreation Site that drops down to the beach. Head south. This is mostly difficult sand, soft and sloped, especially at high tide when there is only a narrow passage for walking between the riprap and the ocean. At 2 miles, about 0.3 mile from where the beach ends at Fishing Rock, get off the beach. This egress is not well marked, but it becomes Willow Street. Do not get off the beach before Willow Street, because those streets will lead to the highway sooner than you need to get there (although there are sidewalks along this portion of the highway).

Walk the mile to Fogarty Creek State Recreation Area by turning right (south) off Willow Street to Evergreen Avenue, and follow that street several blocks until it ends at Lincoln Avenue. Turn left, and left again on Fishing Rock Street to reach US Highway 101. Turn right and walk a short distance on the sidewalk until the north access of Fogarty Creek State Recreation Area is visible across the highway. Cross the highway carefully and head downhill along the edge of the park road. The distance covered so far is 3 miles.

Once in the park, cross a small bridge over Fogarty Creek and follow the path toward the beach, passing under the highway. Do not get on the

Day 14: Gleneden Beach State Recreation Site to Devils Punchbowl State Natural Area

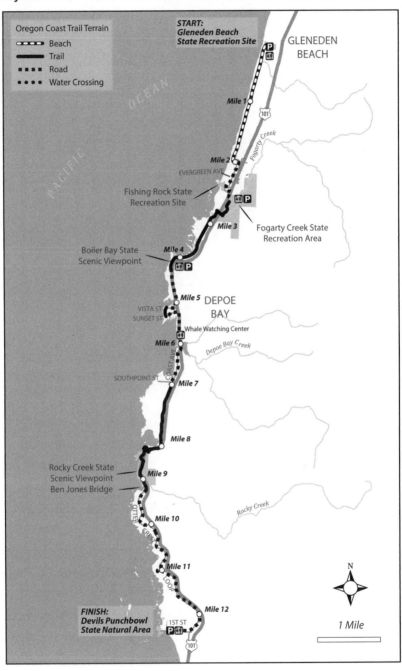

beach; rather, walk up the stairs to the highway to find a trail that parallels it—sometimes above, sometimes below, and at times just on the other side of the guardrail. After a while, it goes deeper into the forest, emerging after 1.8 miles at Boiler Bay State Scenic Viewpoint.

The boiler of Boiler Bay is still visible at extreme low tides. Here, a woman poses in front of it, 1940. (Oregon Historical Society Research Library, bb012860)

The viewpoint overlooks Boiler Bay, which was so named when a ship ran aground in the bay (then known as Brigg's Landing) on May 18, 1910, after a fire spread throughout the engine room, causing the fuel tanks to explode. The remains of the vessel were left in the bay, including her engine boiler. Today, the boiler can still be seen at extreme low tides.

From here, walk the sidewalk into Depoe Bay. At NW Harney Street (just past the very large time-share complex), turn right, make an immediate left turn onto Spencer Avenue, and then a right onto NW Vista Street. In a few blocks, where Vista Street intersects with Alsea Avenue, take a grassy public footpath leading to the North Point Pedestrian Loop, which heads south along a low bluff for 0.4 mile, offering amazing views to the north of Pirate Cove with its secret caves. To the south, waves materialize

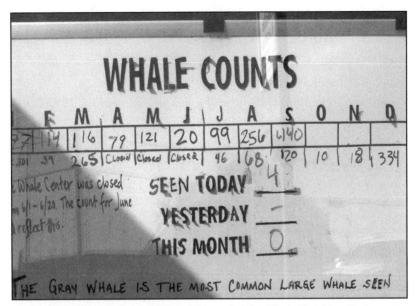

An ongoing count of whale sightings is posted at the Whale Watching Center.

out of nothing to crash against the rocks. Exit the path where it ends at NW Sunset Street and follow that road back to town. Turn right at the highway and continue walking south along the sidewalk.

One of Oregon's more unusual state parks is the Whale Watching Center in Depoe Bay, located on the west side of the highway in the center of town. The center is staffed with rangers and volunteers knowledgeable about whales and other aspects of marine biology. Binoculars are provided for visitors, and a powerful camera focused on whale activity at sea allows for excellent viewing on monitors inside the center. An ongoing count is kept of whale sightings, and the center is visited by as many as 1,500 people a day during peak migrating seasons. It's well worth a brief digression to visit.

Cross the Conde McCullough–designed bridge (the first of several crossed on the OCT) and, toward the end of town, turn right on Ellingson Street, followed by an immediate left onto SW Coast Drive. Follow this scenic road 0.5 mile to Beach Street and turn left. Where Beach and S Point Streets intersect, find the narrow trail that parallels the west side of the highway (at times very close yet separated from the highway) and continue 1.2 miles to Rocky Creek State Scenic Viewpoint. The last stretch of trail leading to the viewpoint offers lovely scenery. From here, walk a short distance along the highway shoulder until reaching Otter Crest Loop, which you'll walk for 4 miles.

Shortly after turning onto the road, hikers will cross another McCullough Bridge.

· ·

The Ben Jones Bridge was constructed on the Oregon Coast Highway in 1927. The highway has since been moved inland slightly, and the bridge now connects to Otter Crest Loop. It spans a small but scenic gorge next to the ocean. This structure was originally called the Rocky Creek Bridge but was subsequently named for Ben Jones, the "Father of the Coast Highway." While serving as state representative for Benton County, Jones advocated for the development of the Oregon Coast Highway, and in 1919 he wrote the first bill authorizing the construction of the highway. Subsequently, Oregon voters authorized funding for its construction, and work on it began in 1921.

· ·

The first 2 miles along the road are uphill through woods and shade. Some of the road shoulder is narrow, and some has a well-established bike path. At Cape Foulweather the road descends for the next 2 miles. Turn right on 1st Street and walk another 0.5 mile to reach Devils Punchbowl State Natural Area.

Conde B. McCullough
and Oregon's Coastal Bridges

OCT HIKERS WALK OVER SEVERAL BRIDGES DESIGNED BY CONDE McCULLOUGH, including the Depoe Bay Bridge (Day 14), the Ben Jones Bridge (Day 14), the Yaquina Bay Bridge (Day 16), the McCullough Memorial Bridge over Coos Bay (Day 25), and the Rogue River Bridge (Day 36). As this guide does not suggest walking through Florence, you will not cross the Siuslaw River Bridge.

You will also cross the new Alsea Bay Bridge on Day 17. It opened in 1991 to replace an original McCullough bridge that had deteriorated and could not be repaired. The replacement was built in a style similar to the original, including an arch that has no structural purpose but mimics the original design. The Alsea Bay Historic Interpretive Center in Waldport was constructed by the Oregon Department of Transportation as part of the bridge replacement project. The center is operated by OPRD and the Waldport Chamber of Commerce, and it houses photographs and other historic memorabilia about the coastal bridges. Its staff leads tours of the Alsea Bay Bridge during summer months.

Building the Oregon Coast Highway

With the completion of the Oregon Coast Highway, coastal communities were better connected with each other and the rest of the state. Prior to 1913, when the Oregon Highway Commission was established, roads were primarily built within towns rather than between them, and only incrementally as funding became available; no central highway plan existed to unify the local roads system. By the 1920s, as automobiles were more affordable and prevalent, Oregonians expressed a clear demand for a better road system.

In 1919 Oregon became the first state to enact a gas tax to fund its roads, and legislation was passed to authorize sale of bonds for a coastal highway. Work on the highway began in 1921, but it would take over ten years to complete it.

Travelers needed formal or informal ferry systems to make connections between communities separated by water. For years, the ferries were privately operated, but they were not always reliable or timely. As a result, public agencies also began operating ferry service. While some of the vessels could accommodate autos, capacity was often limited to ten or fifteen automobiles at a time. As the use of cars became more common, ferry service had to be expanded to meet the demand and was costly to maintain. In 1935, thirty-five automobile ferries operated on waterways throughout Oregon; some of these were privately owned toll ferries, while others were operated by counties or the state.

The last step in completing the highway system was the construction of coastal bridges. Public ferry service was discontinued altogether in 1936 with the opening of five bridges along the Oregon Coast.

McCullough's Bridges

The magnificent bridges designed by Conde McCullough are characterized by their blending of cutting-edge (at the time) engineering techniques with McCullough's appreciation for aesthetics and the natural beauty of their sites. About the Yaquina Bay Bridge, McCullough observed: "Located almost at the mouth of the Yaquina Bay, the Yaquina Bay Bridge has one of the most beautiful and spectacular settings imaginable. Taking advantage of such a setting, a structure in keeping with it has been designed and is being constructed." Here was an engineer with the soul of a poet.

Walking across the bridges at a leisurely pace provides the ability to more closely examine their unique designs and features, a luxury not possible when traveling in a car at 50 miles per hour. The bridges not only allow for pedestrians but were in fact designed to *invite* walkers by including features such as pedestrian plazas and benches. McCullough intended for people to stop to admire the view, and he often designed bridges to include

Public ferries such as this one operated until 1936, when coastal bridges were completed. (Photo 3163 provided by Lincoln County Historical Society)

stairways leading from the bridge to park-like settings. One of the most wonderful features of many of McCullough's bridges is that one can walk under their supportive structures, as is the case with the Yaquina, Siuslaw, Depoe Bay, and McCullough Memorial (Coos Bay) Bridges. Not only is this an opportunity to observe the bridges' underpinnings and magnificent architecture from a unique perspective, but it also often eliminates the need to cross a busy street or highway.

Conde McCullough's career in Oregon lasted nearly thirty years. From 1919, when he moved from Iowa to become the state bridge engineer for the Oregon State Highway Commission, until his death in 1946, McCullough designed and oversaw the construction of some six hundred bridges, but his legacy remains the beautiful bridges along the Oregon Coast Highway that he called "jeweled clasps in a wonderful string of matched pearls."

DAY 15

Devils Punchbowl State Natural Area to Yaquina Bay State Recreation Site

Distance: 9.8 miles

Terrain: Beach, road, highway

Begin: Devils Punchbowl State Natural Area

Directions: From US Highway 101 South, turn west on Otter Crest Loop between mileposts 132 and 133 and follow signs to Devils Punchbowl.

From US Highway 101 North, turn west between mileposts 129 and 130 and follow Otter Crest Loop to 1st Street; turn left and follow it to the parking area on the right.

End: Yaquina Bay State Recreation Site

Directions: From US Highway 101, turn west between mileposts 141 and 142, and follow signs to Yaquina Bay State Recreation Site, which is immediately north of the Yaquina Bay Bridge. Proceed to a parking area below the lighthouse.

Overview

This hike is highlighted by two long and excellent stretches of beach walking interrupted only by the need to circumvent Yaquina (pronounced Yack-Win-A) Head.

At 8 miles into the hike, Nye Beach comes into view, which is recognizable by the Newport Visual Arts Center located at a turnaround next to the beach. This is a good place to detour for coffee, a meal, or restrooms. Since established as a tourist community in the late 1890s, Nye Beach has attracted artists, writers, musicians, and scientists, and as such, it has

Looking for agates was, and is, a favorite pastime along Beverly and Agate Beaches. (Photo 924 provided by Lincoln County Historical Society)

acquired a reputation as an artistic center as well as a popular place to vacation in cottages and campgrounds. The Cliff House Hotel, built in 1911, still stands on a Nye Beach sea cliff and is known now as the Sylvia Beach Hotel. Visitors can stay in rooms named for and decorated in the style of famous authors the likes of William Shakespeare, Agatha Christie, or Gertrude Stein.

Description

Begin the hike by taking a set of stairs across the road from the Devils Punchbowl parking area leading down to the shore. Head south and walk on the beach for 5 miles, crossing numerous shallow streams and rivulets. This beach (Beverly Beach) provides good walking sand. For the patient, it is also a good place for finding agates or fossils. During the winter, rocks embedded with fossil clams and snail shells wash up onto the beach or into streams.

Nearing the headland, wooden steps lead down from a steep slope to the beach from a large private motor coach resort. Just past the stairs and at the end of the beach area, look for (there may be footprints or poles in the sand) a trail that leads up the hillside and turns into a path through the woods leading to either NW 57th or NW 58th Street, depending on which fork in the trail you take. Either way, upon emerging from the trail, turn right onto NW Rhododendron Street and left on NW 55th Street, and walk the few blocks back to the highway. Turn right and walk along the ample shoulder of the highway for less than 0.1 mile until it intersects with NW Lighthouse Drive, where there's a beach-access parking area and trail leading to the sand.

Continue walking south along the beach for another 4 miles, past the north end of Newport. Pass a row of uninspired hotel architecture along the ridge and head toward the jetty. The red dome of the Yaquina Bay Lighthouse and the observation deck next to it may be visible through the trees. Just before the jetty, a trail leads through the shallow dunes to a set of concrete stairs heading up to the parking area.

• •

The Yaquina Bay Lighthouse was built in 1871 and decommissioned just three years later when a new lighthouse was built nearby on Yaquina Point. It had the shortest duration of active duty of any lighthouse on the coast. The Coast Guard later used the lighthouse until 1933, when it was again abandoned. The lighthouse and adjacent lands were transferred to the State of Oregon in 1934 (thank you, Samuel Boardman) for public highway and park purposes. In 1974, Oregon State Parks initiated a yearlong, thorough restoration of the lighthouse and had it listed on the National Register of Historic Places. The lighthouse is the only existing wooden lighthouse in Oregon and is believed to be the oldest structure in Newport. It is open to the public and can be toured daily year-round.

• •

DAY 16

Yaquina Bay State Recreation Site to Seal Rock State Recreation Site

Distance: 10.5 miles

Terrain: Road, trail, beach

Begin: Yaquina Bay State Recreation Site

Directions: From US Highway 101, turn west between mileposts 141 and 142, and follow signs to Yaquina Bay State Recreation Site, which is immediately north of the Yaquina Bay Bridge. Proceed to a parking area below the lighthouse.

End: Seal Rock State Recreation Site

Directions: From US Highway 101, between mileposts 150 and 151, turn west into Seal Rock State Recreation Site and its ample parking area.

Lincoln County Transit provides bus service between Newport and Seal Rock.

Overview

This is a wonderfully diverse hike that begins by walking across and then under the iconic Yaquina Bay Bridge and includes a bit of town walking as well as local trail and beach hiking. At the end of this day, you'll thank your lucky stars you're in Oregon.

Description

Start the hike by following signs leading from the park area to the Yaquina Bay Bridge and cross it single file on the narrow pedestrian walkway. The Yaquina Bay Bridge spans Yaquina Bay and connects Newport to South

OCT hikers can walk under the Yaquina Bay Bridge.

Beach. This is one of Conde McCullough's signature coastal bridges; with its opening on September 6, 1936, state-sponsored ferry services were discontinued and the Oregon Coast Highway system was considered complete.

Walkers have the opportunity that drivers do not have: to appreciate unique features that McCullough incorporated into the bridge's design intended to enhance access for pedestrians. Curved stairways lead up to and down from the bridge, and built-in benches at either end provide a place to sit and enjoy the view.

At the south end of the bridge, walk down the stairs to the park under the bridge, and take a moment to enjoy the intimacy afforded by being able to walk underneath the bridge, picnic in its shadow, or play on its beams. Walk across the grass, cross SW Abalone Street, and turn left onto SW 26th Street, which leads to the south jetty. Here, you are 1 mile into the hike.

In another mile, look for a sign on the left side of the road indicating the South Beach Day-Use Trail. Take this paved trail (the unpaved Old Jetty Trail will also get you there) for 1 mile through the park, following signs to the day-use area, where there are restrooms and picnic tables. Return to the beach here by crossing over a small dune next to the restrooms.

Day 16: Yaquina Bay State Recreation Site to Seal Rock State Recreation Site

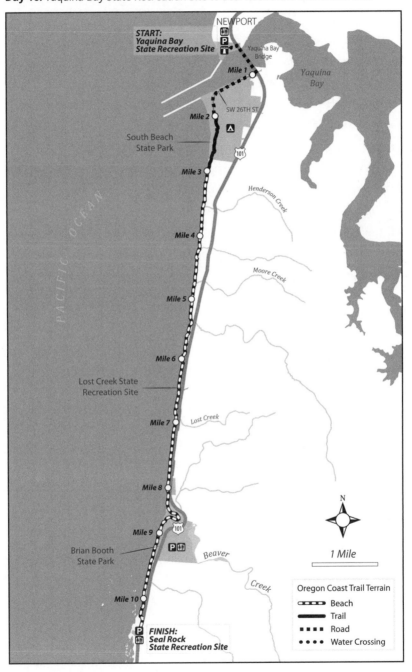

Alternatively, access the beach sooner by following the directional signs along the path.

Continue walking south—this stretch of beach has fewer access points and as a result is less used. Pretty, rose-colored striated cliffs border the beach to the east. Wade a few creeks, the most significant being Beaver Creek at Brian Booth State Park, which is reached after about 5 miles on the beach. If the tide does not allow, or if preferred, follow the beach around to access a trail and bridge crossing over the creek.

Walk another 2 miles on the beach. Seal Rock looms in the distance; however, it is not possible to access the parking area from the north, even during low tide. Take a trail (less than 0.25 mile from the rocks) leading off the beach and up the hillside to US Highway 101. Walk a short distance along the highway shoulder to the parking area at Seal Rock State Recreation Site.

DAY 17

Seal Rock State Recreation Site to Smelt Sands State Recreation Site OR NW Quail Street to Smelt Sands State Recreation Site

Distance: 14.1 miles, 13.1 miles if starting at NW Quail Street

Terrain: Beach, road, trail

Begin: Seal Rock State Recreation Site

Directions: From US Highway 101, between mileposts 150 and 151, turn west into Seal Rock State Recreation Site and its ample parking area.

If beginning at NW Quail Street (high tide), turn west onto NW Quail Street 1 mile south of Seal Rock State Recreation Site. Very limited parking is available.

End: Smelt Sands State Recreation Site

Directions: From US Highway 101, turn west between mileposts 163 and 164 onto Lemwick Lane and proceed 0.2 mile to the parking area.

Lincoln County Transit provides bus service between Seal Rock and Yachats.

Overview

Ideally, begin at Seal Rock just before or at low tide in order to walk around the rock formations. This timing will also ensure you reach Alsea Bay in Waldport, 6 miles into the hike, before high tide. At low tide beautiful tide pools are exposed, abundant with sea urchins and colorful starfish (although, as of 2014, the starfish are mysteriously dying). Oregon's schoolchildren come to Seal Rock by the yellow busload to learn about marine life.

If at Seal Rock the tide is too high to navigate the rock formations, start the hike at the foot of NW Quail Street 1 mile south, where the beach is accessed again beyond the rocks. Very limited parking is available here.

While the distance for this hike, just over 14 miles, is longer than most of the other hikes, the walking is not difficult, as it covers two stretches of hard-sand beach, between Seal Rock and Waldport and between Waldport and Yachats. There are also places to stop along the way for a picnic lunch or to otherwise enjoy a respite. You can shorten the hike by ending at Waldport (6 miles) or at Governor Patterson Memorial State Recreation Site, at about 7 miles.

You will cross numerous creeks along the way, so wear walking sandals or waterproof shoes, or otherwise be prepared to take your shoes and socks off six or seven times.

Description

Option 1—Low or lower tides: At lower tides, begin the hike at Seal Rock State Recreation Site by walking down the paved path on the south side of the wayside, to the left of the restrooms. Upon reaching the beach, walk south until reaching the first rock outcropping. At low tide, it's possible to walk around and through the rock formations. Or look for a low rock shelf at the base of the cliffs just below the highway with a well-defined path leading through the rocks. Continue south to a second rock formation; walk around it if possible or scramble over it if necessary.

Option 2—High tide: If the tides do not allow passage at Seal Rock, begin the hike at the foot of NW Quail Street, a mile south. The rest of the hike is the same for both options.

The beach widens here and extends far ahead. On a foggy day, the outlook is ethereal and mysterious, with the looming shapes of massive rocks on sand shrouded by mist. Continue walking at the ocean's edge.

At about 4.4 miles from Seal Rock, leave the beach in Waldport at the Bayshore Beach Club (on NW Oceania Drive), which is marked with a short wooden post painted yellow at the edge of the grasses, possibly making it hard to spot from the beach. But any of the sandy pathways from the

Day 17: Seal Rock State Recreation Site to Smelt Sands State Recreation Site

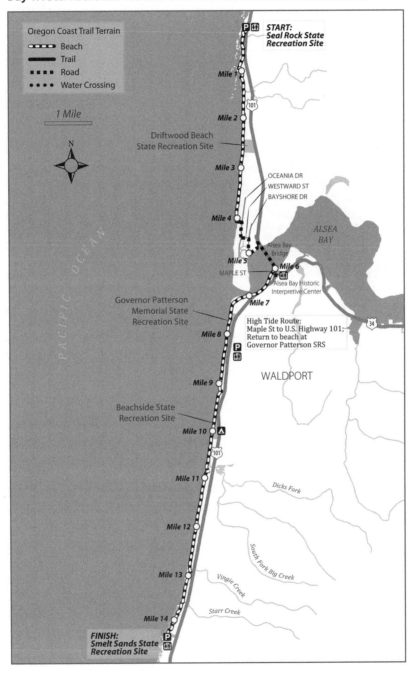

The Alsea Bay Bridge north wayside leads to the new bridge and displays pylons from the original structure.

beach to the road between miles 4 and 4.4 will take you to NW Oceania Drive.GPS coordinates for exiting the beach at Bayshore Beach Club: N 44°26.218', W 124°05.078'.

Get onto Westward Street, directly in front of the Bayshore Beach Club. Walk east a couple of short blocks and then right on NW Bayshore Drive, taking it until it ends in about 0.25 mile at a private development on the Alsea River.

Follow the Alsea River shoreline east, and in 0.2 mile, just before you're under the Alsea Bay Bridge, take a short, old, paved path uphill. This path once served as a ferry dock. It's overgrown and a little rough but not difficult. It emerges in 0.1 mile at the Alsea Bay Bridge north wayside. Turn into the wayside, the site of the north entrance to the original McCullough-designed Alsea Bay Bridge, which was replaced in 1991. Take a close-up look at some decorative pylons from that original bridge, which have been installed at the plaza, and then walk up the steps to the bridge, which has a nice pedestrian pathway to the other side.

Restrooms and water are available at the Alsea Bay Historic Interpretive Center located at the foot of the bridge on the south side of the river. It

Seawall at Waldport: Do not try this at high tide.

also houses interesting displays and photos about Oregon's coastal bridges, and staff provides tours of the bridge during the summer months. From there, get onto the beach and head south. Ideally, this portion of the hike, reached at about 6 miles, should also be approached near low or mid-tide, or at least not at high tide, since the beach between the bay and the re-taining wall is very narrow or nonexistent during high tide.

High Tide Route: If an alternate route is necessary, follow Maple Street in front of the interpretive center until it joins with US Highway 101 and then walk along the highway shoulder 0.5 mile to Governor Patterson Memorial State Recreation Site, where there is beach access. Local trail advocates have developed an alternative high-tide route that will eliminate almost all highway walking. A new trail, scheduled for construction in 2015, will take hikers on the east side of the highway, across the highway, and through local streets until dropping down to the beach again.

Continue south on the beach for nearly 8 miles, passing Beachside State Recreation Site. Occasionally, you may catch a glimpse of traffic along US Highway 101, but the low bluffs, windswept trees, and other coastal vegetation provide enough of a barrier that, for the most part, the road cannot be seen or heard. Continue walking south, crossing a few streams and creeks. Near Yachats, the beach ends and the shoreline transitions into a rocky plateau. The 804 Trail begins here; follow it up a slope and continue another 0.75 mile to Smelt Sands State Recreation Site by turning left on a gravel path leading into the parking area.

Yachats 804 Trail

AS WAS THE CASE ELSEWHERE ALONG THE COAST, THOSE WHO CAME TO settle near Yachats—and the Native American populations before them—had used the beach for transportation for many years. The eight miles between Waldport and Yachats were traveled on sand until the beach ends at the basalt shelf where Yachats begins. Travelers continuing south left the beach to continue on a road established along the ocean bluff.

In the late 1890s, the route was designated as County Road 804. In 1916 County Road 802 was built farther inland—eventually to be rebuilt as the Roosevelt Coast Military Highway, which today is US Highway 101—and county maintenance of County Road 804 ceased. Property on the bluff was eventually settled and became privately owned, but travelers still were allowed to cross the land to continue their journeys. The road continued to be used by vehicle traffic as well as pedestrians enjoying the oceanfront walk.

In the 1970s, a long legal battle regarding the trail's usage began. Several property owners in Yachats petitioned the Lincoln County commissioners to "vacate" the road. Essentially, they sought to eliminate County Road 804 from county maps in order to claim it as part of their own property. Those favoring this action claimed they were unable to use or develop portions of their own property, that the assumed right-of-way was not the same as the path used by the public, and that many people were trespassing. As a result, some property owners built fences blocking access to the trail. Complicated legal proceedings continued for several years. The state attorney general issued a decision that the road was to be considered vacated—and then rescinded that decision.

This was County Road 804 in 1892. (Photo 1188 provided by Lincoln County Historical Society)

A group of local citizens organized as Save the Yachats 804 Trail and submitted an application for the road to be placed on the National Register of Historic Places, based on the history and continued use of the trail, but they were not successful. However, the group became active in advocating for continued use of the trail. They were supported in their legal efforts by 1000 Friends of Oregon. In 1978, the state parks agency went on record, through the Oregon Recreation Trails Advisory Council, to endorse the "maintenance of a public right-of-way as an important part of the Oregon Coast Trail."

In 1979, the case to vacate the trail was brought before the Lincoln County Circuit Court. The court ruled against the landowners in preserving not only the right-of-way but also some of the adjacent private land, which was determined to be public because of years of common and uninterrupted use. The landowners appealed to the higher Oregon courts, but the lower court decision was upheld.

Dave Talbot, superintendent of state parks and recreation from 1964 to 1992, recollected the state's involvement, or initial lack of involvement, in preserving the 804 Trail this way:

> I've long regretted the fact we didn't pick up that cause earlier. It should have been a Parks cause to protect that old right-of-way, but we ducked it at first.... After the case was upheld by a ruling of the Oregon Supreme Court in 1985, State Parks agreed to take

Today, the 804 Trail is an integral part of the Oregon Coast Trail.

over the right-of-way and develop it for a hiking trail. We have that valuable addition to the coastal trail system thanks to determined citizen activists who knew what was right.

Those landowners who had erected fences, hedges, or other obstacles preventing access to the right-of-way were asked to voluntarily remove them; none did. As a result, the State Parks Department tore down the barriers on the grounds that unimpeded access to the 804 Trail was an integral part of the Oregon Coast Trail.

A similar legal battle over the south end of the trail began in the 1990s and was finally settled through mediation with the bordering homeowners. Now the trail extends from Smelt Sands State Recreation Site south to the Yachats River.

Today it is difficult to imagine that an old road slightly more than a mile in length could have been the subject of so much controversy and contention. In fact, the 804 Trail is highlighted on the Yachats Chamber of Commerce website as a scenic attraction in Yachats, and some hotels fronting the trail offer brochures and maps about it. The spectacular and uninterrupted views afforded along the 804 Trail are enjoyed by everyone rather than being limited to those few fortunate enough to own property along the ridge.

DAY 18

Smelt Sands State Recreation Site
to Cummins Creek Trailhead

Distance: 8.6 miles

Terrain: Trail, road, highway

Begin: Smelt Sands State Recreation Site

Directions: From US Highway 101, turn west between mileposts 163 and 164 onto Lemwick Lane and proceed 0.2 mile to the parking area.

End: Cummins Creek Trailhead (not to be confused with Cummins Ridge Trail)

Directions: From US Highway 101, turn east between mileposts 168 and 169 at the Cummins Creek Trailhead sign, immediately north of a small bridge and the Neptune Day-Use Area.

Overview

Even though you are not on sand at all today, dramatic ocean views abound, especially for the first part of the walk along the 804 Trail, which traverses a scenic bluff above the ocean. Thanks to an active cadre of local volunteers, the trail is meticulously signed along the way and so avoids what could be a complicated hike with its many zigs and zags. The City of Yachats and various civic organizations have also conveniently provided benches at numerous spots all through town, especially along Ocean View Drive. Another highlight is visiting Amanda's Grotto on the lower flanks of Cape Perpetua and traversing the scenic trails on the cape.

The total elevation gain for this hike is 1,702 feet, and the total elevation loss is 1,551 feet.

Description

Start the hike at the Smelt Sands State Recreation Site and turn left onto the path from the parking area, which is the 804 Trail. Continue south, behind the hotels and resorts on the cliff, and then follow Oregon Coast Trail markers directing hikers to a path on mowed grass between two fences. This leads to Marine Drive, which turns into Ocean View Drive. Walk this road 1 mile to Yachats State Recreation Area. Continue to follow Ocean View Drive as it curves along the river all the way to the highway. Cross over the Yachats River using the pedestrian access on the bridge. Walk along the shoulder of US Highway 101 for 0.25 mile until reaching Yachats Ocean Road on the right. Follow it as it turns to the left and, just before reaching US Highway 101 again, look for OCT markers to the right. For the next 0.2 mile, the path parallels the highway just inside the guardrail. At Windy Way Street, reached 2.5 miles into the hike, cross the highway carefully and look for a trail with an OCT sign peeking through the woods.

Amanda's Trail starts as a moderate path just above and next to the highway. It soon enters the forest and crosses a footbridge over a stream. After 0.75 mile, hikers reach the Amanda Grotto—a lush, serene, and contemplative spot. Amanda's statue is placed below the bridge; she is often adorned with beads and forest moss, feathers, and other gifts of nature. Take a moment for reflection at the grotto, and read about her story and how this trail got its name.

The next segment, from the Amanda Grotto to the Cape Perpetua Visitor Center, is 3.9 miles. After crossing the bridge, the trail begins a relentless uphill for about 0.75 mile, without the benefit of switchbacks, then mercifully levels out or at least climbs more gradually. Here, deep in the woods, it is quiet except for the occasional sound of the creek. Upon reaching a fork in the road at the top of the trail, turn right and continue on the wooded path that offers outstanding views and terminates at the parking area. The well-marked St. Perpetua Trail leads to the Cape Perpetua Visitor Center. (At the road at the campground, turn left and pick up the trail again in a few yards.) The terrain is mostly downhill, with a brief uphill as you reach the center. A paved path (Captain Cook

Day 18: Smelt Sands State Recreation Site to Cummins Creek Trailhead

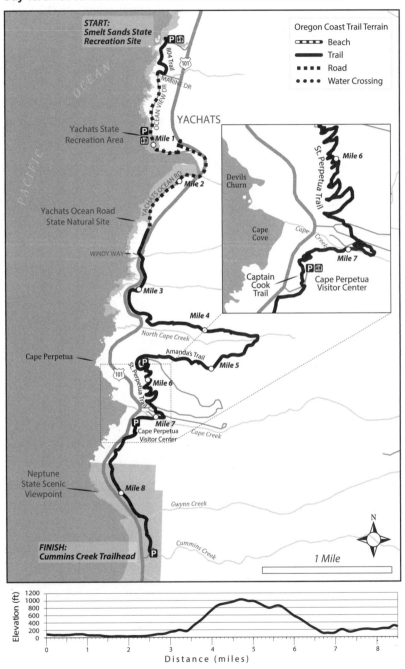

Trail) in front of the visitor center soon converges into the OCT on the left-hand side. Continue south for 1.5 miles, crossing Gwynn Creek, to reach the Cummins Creek Trailhead.

Plans are underway to extend the trail another 1.5 miles to Bob Creek, but for now the OCT here directs hikers to the highway for most of the next 6.5 miles, interrupted only by a short beach walk. This stretch of the highway provides little if any shoulder for much of the way, and I recommend it be skipped.

Amanda's Trail

AMANDA'S TRAIL ALLOWS FOR A SEAMLESS CONNECTION OF THE OREGON Coast Trail from the south side of Yachats to the top of Cape Perpetua. As hikers begin to ascend the cape, they walk across private property, which is made possible because of an easement provided by the property owner.

The trail was planned for and constructed in fits and starts over a period of twenty-five years with the support (although at times slow and cumbersome) of several public agencies. Community volunteers and members of the Confederated Tribes of Coos, Lower Umpqua, and Siuslaw Indians also worked together to ensure that a difficult but important chapter of Oregon's history is remembered. To tell the story of the trail is also to tell the story of Amanda herself, for they cannot be separated.

It began when a Forest Service ranger named Loyd Collett attended a lecture by Stephen Dow Beckham, an Oregon historian who conducted extensive research about Native American populations and the history of Indians in and near Yachats in the mid-nineteenth century. Collett learned about the story of Amanda De-Cuys, a member of the Coos Tribe, who, when her common-law husband refused to marry her, was forced to leave her daughter in May 1864 and march with dozens of members of the Coos and Lower Umpqua Tribes from Coos Bay to Yachats, where they were interred. One of the soldiers, Corporal Royal Bensell, kept a diary of his experiences, writing that the blind and elderly Amanda "tore her feet horribly over these ragged rock, leaving blood sufficient to track her by."

As documented by Beckham in his book *The Indians of Western Oregon: This Land was Theirs* and elsewhere, conditions at the reservation—known as the Alsea Subagency and located in part in present-day Yachats—were abysmal, and as a result, thousands of Indians died of disease, starvation, or broken spirits. They were denied their traditional sources of sustenance; their lands were usurped as they were forced to leave their ancestral homes and to abandon traditions, language, and a culture that had flourished for centuries.

Collett was moved enough to name a new trail he had identified that would traverse down the north side of Cape Perpetua as Amanda's Trail.

In 1986, Norman and Joanne Kittel purchased twenty-seven acres of property adjacent to Cape Perpetua. Although they did not begin construction on their residence until 1993 (the Kittels were living in Minnesota when they made the purchase), they were aware of the Oregon Coast Trail and from the beginning wished to provide an easement across their property to facilitate access to the trail. Perhaps not accustomed to property owners actually volunteering an easement, local and federal agencies were at first not sure how to respond. Complicating matters, the land on Cape Perpetua is owned and managed by the United States Forest Service, but the trail is managed by the Oregon Parks and Recreation Department. Ultimately, though, a permanent easement was negotiated with OPRD.

Upon moving to Yachats, Joanne Kittel began to learn about the history of the Native American population in her new home. What began as curiosity led to collaboration with staff and members of the Confederated Tribes of Siletz Indians as well as the Confederated Tribes of Coos, Lower Umpqua, and Siuslaw Indians. Tribal members and staff made field notes and other records available to Joanne and her coauthor, Suzanne Curtis, who collected and reported this information in an article intended to raise awareness of a past the authors believed had been misrepresented or denied altogether. The original article, titled "Early Yachats History: The Yachats Indians, Origins of the Yachats Name, and the Reservation Years," was completed in 1996 and revised in 2010. It is available on the internet at www.yachats.info/history1.htm.

Progress on Amanda's Trail was sporadic. Although it was identified and included in the Forest Service's trail construction plan, lack of funding prevented the agency from actually building it. Furthermore, safety concerns were expressed at constructing a trail that would terminate at the highway. In order to move forward, Joanne Kittel solicited local volunteers to help build the trail by posting a notice on a community bulletin board. In January 1997 volunteers began gathering the first Saturday of every month, and they completed the first segment of the trail that fall. The original Amanda Bridge was built in three days with labor provided by state and federal agency staff, Job Corps students, and community volunteers. The new trail, 2.6 miles from the top of Cape Perpetua through the Kittel property to the highway, was dedicated in 1998.

One of the community members attending that dedication was inspired to donate a statue created by local artist Sy Meadow. In 2003 the Amanda statue was placed along the trail below the bridge. Her presence attracted more interest in the trail and helped advance and expand the knowledge of Amanda's story.

A connection was still needed to link the end of the trail with the town in order to avoid dangerous highway walking. Despite doubts by parks personnel and the Oregon Department of Transportation that a trail could be adequately constructed along the ODOT highway right-of-way, a local landscape architect envisioned and designed a solution that was accepted by the agencies. The City of Yachats received a grant and provided matching funds to complete the trail along the west side of the highway, even though most of it is outside city limits.

The final segment of Amanda's Trail was completed in 2009, and a second dedication took place. Invitations to the dedication were extended to tribal members; over thirty attended, most of them traveling from the Coos Bay area. For many years, Amanda's descendants had refused to come to Yachats, traveling miles out of their way to avoid a place associated with the virtual extermination of their people. But, according to tribal representatives today, the Amanda Grotto is now considered a place of remembrance, a special place where they can—and do—come to pay tribute to their ancestors, a place that helped initiate healing and reconciliation.

In 2010 the Oregon Geographic Names Board was successfully petitioned to name the creek under the bridge Amanda Creek, and in 2011 a

Volunteers helped build the new Amanda Bridge in 2011. (Photo by Greg Scott)

new bridge was built. The Confederated Tribes of Coos, Lower Umpqua, and Siuslaw Indians contributed funds for the project, and tribal members worked side-by-side with local community members to dismantle the old bridge and build the new one.

Recently, a new tradition was born in Yachats. Each New Year's Day, the Yachats Trails Committee sponsors a walk from the community center along the south 804 Trail, across the bridge over the Yachats River, and along Yachats Ocean Road to Amanda's Trail, with the final destination being the Amanda Grotto. At the statue, hikers are invited to participate in a wreath ceremony, to pay tribute to Amanda, and to offer blessings of peace for the new year.

DAY 19

Ocean Beach Picnic Area OR Muriel O. Ponsler Memorial State Scenic Viewpoint to Heceta Head Lighthouse State Scenic Viewpoint

Distance: 5.7 miles on low-tide route or 4.4 miles on other-tides route
Terrain: Beach, trail
Begin: Ocean Beach Picnic Area at low tide only, or Muriel O. Ponsler Memorial State Scenic Viewpoint
Directions: Ocean Beach Picnic Area: From US Highway 101, turn west at the sign for the picnic area, between mileposts 173 and 174. Daily recreation fee, applicable federal recreation pass, or Oregon Pacific Coast Passport is required.

Muriel O. Ponsler Memorial State Scenic Viewpoint: From US Highway 101 turn west at the sign for the viewpoint, between mileposts 175 and 176.

End: Heceta Head Lighthouse State Scenic Viewpoint
Directions: From US Highway 101, turn west at the sign to Heceta Head Lighthouse State Scenic Viewpoint, between mileposts 178 and 179. Daily parking fee, state recreational pass, or Oregon Pacific Coast Passport required.

This guide recommends eliminating highway walking between Cummins Creek and both starting places for this day's hike.

Overview

This is a short and pleasant hike that begins on the beach and ends at Heceta Head Lighthouse. In between, hikers can channel their inner hobbit.

Description

Option 1—low tide: At low tide, and low tide only, it may be possible to start this hike at Ocean Beach Picnic Area, which is managed by the US Forest Service. Walk from the parking area down to the beach and continue south around the rocky headland. Cross Rock Creek and walk 1.3 miles to the Muriel O. Ponsler Memorial State Scenic Viewpoint.

Option 2—other tides: At other tides, which will be most of the time, begin the hike at the Ponsler Viewpoint. Mile points below are based on starting there.

From the Muriel O. Ponsler Memorial State Scenic Viewpoint, walk south on the beach toward Heceta Head, and at about 1.75 miles, look for a wide swath in the sand leading off the beach and onto a trail in the brush. This is the Hobbit Trail. Follow it a little more than 0.5 mile back up close to the highway. The trail heads uphill for most of the time, through a lovely forest—fern laden, mossy, and prolific with gnarly roots. The overhead foliage forms a canopy, conjuring up a mystical fairyland forest. At the trail juncture, turn right and continue south toward the lighthouse on a trail that climbs steadily at first, and steeply at times, through old Sitka spruce and salal for 1.5 miles to Heceta Head Lighthouse. Benches are strategically placed along the route for enjoying the views and allowing some quiet reflection in the woods. The trail continues eastward from the lighthouse then drops down the hill to Heceta Head Lighthouse State Scenic Viewpoint and farther down to the parking area.

• •

Heceta Head Lighthouse is open to the public for tours daily March through October. Allegedly it is the most photographed lighthouse on the Pacific Coast, as it appears in many calendars and on note cards. This active, fifty-six-foot-high lighthouse has a rotating beam that is still the most powerful on the Oregon Coast. Its first-order lens shines twenty-two miles out to sea. The lighthouse needed major repairs a few years ago and was in danger of being deactivated, but funding from the federal transportation department and OPRD (the lighthouse owner) resulted in a major renovation, completed in 2013.

• •

Preserving the Past

THAT THE OCT EXISTS AT ALL IS DUE TO THE PRESENCE OF INDIAN TRAILS developed generations ago and used for transportation or to indicate territorial boundaries—these are paths we still walk today. Despite scientific documentation that Native Americans lived in established communities along the coast for thousands of years, little tangible evidence of this remains. Even before white settlers arrived in the mid-nineteenth century, coastal tribes had been decimated by introduced diseases for which they had no immunity, such as smallpox and tuberculosis.

Once coastal areas became populated by settlers seeking land claims, gold, and other natural resources, Indians were forcibly removed from their homes, and their native sites were systematically destroyed or usurped for other purposes. In 1866, the Coast Guard began operating the Cape Arago Lighthouse, which was built on an island considered sacred by the Coos Indians, where many of their ancestors were buried. Little regard or respect was paid to Native American burial practices or spiritual traditions, as indicated by this passage reported in the recollections of early settler Alexandria Rock, published in her book *History of the Little Nestucca Country*:

> It was the custom of the Nestuggas (Indians) to put their dead Brave in his canoe and swing the canoe between two trees. The earliest settlers, needing canoes, dumped the bones out and took the canoes for their own. Some of the Nestuggas had fine big canoes which they had hewn from cedar logs found washed in on the Beach.

Indian shell middens were once common near what is now Yachats, but they were often destroyed to build roads. (Photo courtesy of OPRD)

Early roads along some parts of the coast, including Yachats, were built with Native American shell middens—middens that sometimes served as burial grounds and now provide us with information about tribal life and customs. But, as reported by the *Lincoln County Leader* in 1909, these middens were destroyed to build roads:

> Down in the Salmon River Country and on the Yachats they have a fine material for road building. Along the beach at these places are acres of shells, put there by the Indians, and it must have taken years—probably centuries—to accumulate such a vast amount. In some places these shells are ten feet deep and cover many acres. There is ample at the mouth of each of these streams to furnish dressing of the finest quality for many miles of road.

The exact location of preserved historical Indian sites is kept confidential, since to publicize them could cause further destruction or promote looting and stealing of artifacts, which routinely occurred in Oregon for decades. Both state and federal laws have been enacted to ensure the protection of archaeological sites, resources, and objects, and it is considered a felony offense to remove, disturb, or destroy any such objects. The first laws in Oregon concerning protection of Indian burial sites were not enacted until the 1970s, and in the mid-1980s regulations were passed to protect other cultural resources.

Present-day guidelines require an assessment for projects (including building or expanding a trail) that may impact a known archaeological site. Prior to the initiation of these activities, the designated archaeologist consults with local tribes regarding the proposed methodology and other aspects of the project. In some cases, tribal archaeologists also participate in the fieldwork. If artifacts of interest are found, the archaeological protocol is to "protect in place"—in other words, to not move or disturb them. Should the presence of artifacts be confirmed on the project site—for example, where a trail is planned—a mitigation plan is developed to avoid the site, perhaps by redirecting the trail around it.

DAY 20

Baker Beach Campground
to Siuslaw River North Jetty

Distance: 5.5 miles

Terrain: Beach

Begin: Baker Beach Campground

Directions: From US Highway 101, at milepost 182, look carefully for a sign indicating Baker Beach Road to the west. Follow the gravel road to the parking area. Daily recreation fee, applicable federal recreation pass, or Oregon Pacific Coast Passport required.

End: Siuslaw River North Jetty Parking Area

Directions: From US Highway 101 in Florence, turn west on Heceta Beach Road between mileposts 187 and 188, left on Rhododendron Drive, and right onto N Jetty Road to the parking area.

This guide recommends eliminating 4 miles between Heceta Head Lighthouse State Scenic Viewpoint and Baker Beach Campground, which would otherwise be walked along US Highway 101 and through a tunnel with no pedestrian access.

Overview

This day offers a very straightforward and quiet beach walk, and is a nice introduction to the dunes.

Description

From the parking area at Baker Beach Campground, which is part of the Siuslaw National Forest, find the well-marked trailhead just west of the restrooms. Walkers share the wide, sandy trail that begins here with horses. Follow it about 0.3 mile over some small dunes and onto the beach. Climbing to the top of one of the dunes adjacent to the beach allows nice views both to the north and the south—on a clear day, all the way to the jetty. This hike provides just a hint of what's to come in the Oregon Dunes National Recreation Area.

This remote section of beach is bordered by the dunes to the east and by the ocean to the west. Head south and continue just over 5 miles, wading Sutton Creek about halfway into the walk, until reaching the north jetty of the Siuslaw River. Upon reaching the jetty, turn inland and follow it to the Siuslaw River north jetty parking area.

The densely forested trail over Tillamook Head is believed to be virtually the same route used by members of the Lewis and Clark Expedition in January 1806 when they traveled with the guidance of their Indian scout and translator Sacajawea in search of a beached whale. (Photo by Frank Harris)

Indian Beach, in Ecola State Park, is a favored spot for surfing. Hikers arrive at Indian Beach after traversing Tillamook Head. From here the OCT continues into Cannon Beach.

Beautiful and colorful tide pools are exposed at low tide near Cannon Beach. However, the starfish population has been infected with a virus causing sea star wasting syndrome, which has resulted in many starfish dying along Oregon shores.

You can hail a boat taxi to transport you from the end of Nehalem Spit to Jetty Fishery. This is the first of several boat rides along the OCT that save miles of unpleasant highway walking.

Three trails converge in Cape Lookout State Park. You will take the North Trail to reach the top of the cape and then the South Trail to get back on the beach toward Sand Lake.

The scenery in and near Depoe Bay is dramatic because of its rocky shoreline. It is a great place to hunker down and watch winter storms. (Gary Halvorson, Oregon State Archives)

The Rocky Creek Bridge, also known as the Ben Jones Bridge, was completed in 1927. It spans a small scenic gorge near Depoe Bay and is one of many bridges designed by Conde McCullough. Those hiking the entire OCT will have the opportunity to walk across several of McCullough's elegant coastal bridges.

An Oregon State Park ranger teaches about marine life at Seal Rock. On Day 17, you will begin hiking at Seal Rock and walk all the way to Yachats.

OCT hikers will traverse Amanda's Trail on scenic Cape Perpetua. The trail was named for a member of the Coos Indian Tribe who was forcibly removed from her home and taken to the Alsea Subagency on the Coast Reservation near Yachats, which was established to "manage" Indians who lived between Coos Bay and the Alsea River. This statue represents Amanda and has been placed next to the trail.

Here are two hikers on the John Dellenback Dunes Trail. The trail is named for Oregon Congressman John Dellenback, who facilitated an agreement to designate the Oregon Dunes National Recreation Area in 1972. (Photo by Carolyn Ableman)

Plan on lingering in the formal and beautiful gardens at Shore Acres State Park. The Oregon Coast Trail passes by this lily pond. (Gary Halvorson, Oregon State Archives)

The long stretch of beach between China Creek and Floras Lake is especially remote and good for beachcombing.

OCT hikers can visit several scenic and historic lighthouses along the route. Cape Blanco is the most southern of Oregon's lighthouses and is the westernmost point in Oregon. (Gary Halvorson, Oregon State Archives)

The hikes through the Samuel H. Boardman State Scenic Corridor are among the most spectacular of the entire journey. Here is Lone Ranch Beach, which is part of the Oregon Coast Trail. (Gary Halvorson, Oregon State Archives)

In 1967, Governor Tom McCall signed the Beach Bill into law, which designated the "dry sands" as a recreational area. As a result, Oregon is one of only three states that allow public access to their entire shoreline.

This portrait hangs in the capitol building in Salem and surely serves as one of the more unorthodox official governor portraits anywhere: Tom McCall looming large, extending a hand, with one foot in the water and one foot in the (dry) sand. A helicopter hovers in the background, and a survey pole—a symbol of the controversy—is prominent. The portrait seems to capture McCall's charismatic personality, innate political instincts, and effective use of the media—certainly, as a former newscaster himself, he was no stranger to a good photo opportunity.

McCall was Oregon's thirtieth governor, serving from 1967 to 1975. (Gary Halvorson, Oregon State Archives)

DAYS 21–30

Florence to Bandon

Overview

These hikes include four days (Days 21–24) through the dunes—really *through* the dunes. The Oregon Dunes National Recreation Area (ODNRA) is part of the Siuslaw National Forest and is composed of two long stretches of beach (each about 20 miles) between Florence and Winchester Bay, and between Winchester Bay and Coos Bay. The official OCT remains on the beach this entire time, which would require extremely long hiking days if uninterrupted. Furthermore, you would miss out on experiencing the real magic of the dunes by walking next to them but not crossing through them.

Therefore, this guide suggests digressing from the official trail by walking through the dunes on trails between the beach and public waysides, thereby creating four shorter day hikes. This approach adds some distance, as it requires retracing steps on two occasions to resume the hikes, but it's worth it. It is highly recommended that you arrange for a boat shuttle at the end of Day 22 into Winchester Bay.

Day 25 consists of road walking from Horsfall Beach into Ferry Road Park in North Bend and includes crossing the magnificent McCullough Memorial Bridge spanning Coos Bay. The recently completed Sawmill & Tribal Trail between North Bend and the historic Empire District of Coos Bay is included as Day 26. Although the Sawmill & Tribal Trail is not officially incorporated into the OCT, the route is more interesting than the official trail, as it provides interpretive information specific to the tribal history of the area as well as other local historical points of reference.

Seastacks and caves on Bandon's beach are fun to explore at low tide.

You'll visit a beautiful trio of state parks—Sunset Bay, Shore Acres, and Cape Arago— on Day 27. They are linked by trails that traverse the parks and offer spectacular vantage points for views. Plan to linger a bit at Shore Acres in order to better wander through the formal gardens.

Currently, no direct link connects Cape Arago to the beach, so on Day 28 you will backtrack to walk along a scenic and hilly road that leads into Seven Devils State Recreation Site. Day 29 begins at Seven Devils and ends at Bullards Beach State Park—lower tides allow hikers to walk this whole day on the beach, but a very satisfying high-tide alternative is also available. The last hike in this section begins at Bullards Beach State Park and traverses the waterfront of Bandon, reentering the beach at the Coquille River south jetty. This is one of the most scenic beaches along the entire coastline, as it is lined with seastacks and secret caves.

You can enjoy the charms and support the local economies of Florence, Winchester Bay, North Bend, Charleston, and Bandon during this segment of the OCT.

Table 5. Days 21–30: Florence to Bandon

Day	Hike	Miles	Terrain	Considerations
21	Siuslaw River South Jetty to Oregon Dunes Day Use Area	13	Beach, trail	low tide
22	Oregon Dunes Day Use Area to Winchester Bay OR Sparrow Park Road	13.7 or 7.2*	Trail, beach	boat ride optional
23	Winchester Bay to John Dellenback Dunes Trailhead	9.5	Road, beach, trail	
24	John Dellenback Dunes Trailhead to Horsfall Beach	11.5	Trail, beach	
25	Horsfall Beach to Ferry Road Park	5.5	Road, highway	
26	Ferry Road Park to Charleston Marina	10.9	Road, trail,	
27	Charleston to Cape Arago SP	7.5	Road, beach, trail	
28	South Slough National Estuarine Research Reserve to Seven Devils SRS	7.1	Road	
29	Seven Devils SRS to Bullards Beach SP	5.5 or 8.1**	Beach, trail	low tide
30	Bullards Beach SP to China Creek	8.7	Trail, highway, road, beach	

*Hike distance depends on whether boat ride is taken.
**Hike distance is based on tidal considerations.

Days 21–30: South Central Coast Overview

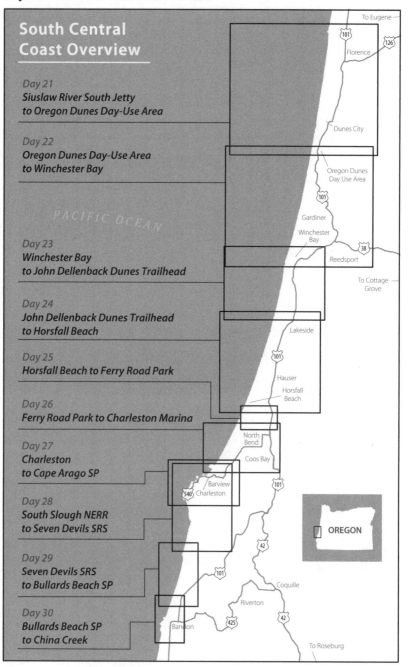

South Central
Coast Overview

Day 21
**Siuslaw River South Jetty
to Oregon Dunes Day-Use Area**

Day 22
**Oregon Dunes Day-Use Area
to Winchester Bay**

Day 23
**Winchester Bay
to John Dellenback Dunes Trailhead**

Day 24
**John Dellenback Dunes Trailhead
to Horsfall Beach**

Day 25
Horsfall Beach to Ferry Road Park

Day 26
Ferry Road Park to Charleston Marina

Day 27
**Charleston
to Cape Arago SP**

Day 28
**South Slough NERR
to Seven Devils SRS**

Day 29
**Seven Devils SRS
to Bullards Beach SP**

Day 30
**Bullards Beach SP
to China Creek**

PACIFIC OCEAN

To Eugene
101
Florence
126
Dunes City
Oregon Dunes
Day Use Area
101
Gardiner
Winchester
Bay
38
Reedsport
To Cottage
Grove
Lakeside
101
Hauser
Horsfall
Beach
North
Bend
Coos Bay
Barview
540 Charleston
101
42
OREGON
Coquille
Riverton
Bandon
425
42
To Roseburg

Oregon Dunes National Recreation Area

National Seashore or National Recreation Area?

THE OREGON DUNES NATIONAL RECREATION AREA CONSISTS OF FORTY miles of the largest expanse of coastal sand dunes in North America and is managed by the United States Forest Service as part of the Siuslaw National Forest. This forest encompasses more than 630,000 acres in total and also includes the Sand Lake Recreation Area and Cape Perpetua. The Oregon Dunes National Recreation Area stretches from the south jetty of the Siuslaw River in Florence to the Umpqua River and from Winchester Bay to Coos Bay.

The Oregon Dunes were set aside as a federally designated recreational area in 1972, culminating twelve years of contentious debate over the area's future, marked by dissention among Oregon's congressional delegation and other elected officials, including then Governor Mark Hatfield. At the heart of the dispute was whether the dunes should be considered a national seashore and overseen by the National Park Service.

In 1959, at the recommendation of the federal parks agency, Oregon Senator Richard Neuberger first introduced legislation proposing the dunes be considered a national seashore. The park area would have included the privately owned Sea Lion Caves as well as three existing state parks, including Jessie M. Honeyman Memorial State Park. At the time, land proposed for the park was under the jurisdiction of numerous agencies, including the Bureau of Land Management, the US Forest Service, the War Department, the Oregon State Highway Commission, local counties, and some private ownership. With the national seashore proposal, all of these various landowners would have been consolidated under the National Park Service and administered by that agency.

Some private property owners within the proposed park area raised concerns that they could lose their property if a national park were designated. This and other issues caused Hatfield and Oregon's other senator, Wayne Morse, to oppose the legislation. (Morse and Neuberger also were engaged in a longstanding bitter personal and political feud, which some claim impaired their ability to effectively collaborate.)

In January 1960, Neuberger submitted revised legislation based on efforts to address these objections. At that time he stated:

> I think the best way to get that park is for Governor Hatfield and me to reach all possible agreement on the details of the legislation authorizing such a national park. Many years from now, the important and essential thing will be the existence of a great national park along America's most majestic shoreline—it will not be what politician salved his vanity or pride by feuding with another politician over whether or not the park should be established. My goal is not political warfare; it is to bring Oregon its first new national park since Crater Lake was set aside in 1902.

Neuberger died in office in March 1960; in November, his widow, Maurine, was elected senator. She carried on his effort to establish a national park, but the authorizing legislation was defeated twelve years in a row.

Oregon Congressman John Dellenback, who represented Oregon's fourth congressional district between 1966 and 1974, finally facilitated a compromise. His bill designated the dunes as a national recreation area and was signed into law by President Richard Nixon in 1972. The agreement differed from the original proposal in several ways—it excluded state parks, left the management of the area to the Forest Service rather than the National Park Service, and allowed for continued private ownership within the recreational area, so long as usage was consistent with Forest Service policies.

The Oregon Dunes National Recreation Area was dedicated and opened to the public on July 15, 1972. In 2004, the wonderful trail through the dunes that you will hike on Days 23 and 24 was renamed from the Umpqua Dunes Trail to the John Dellenback Dunes Trail.

Challenges Today

Today, a number of challenges face the Siuslaw National Forest, which is charged with protecting the Oregon Dunes. Chief among these challenges is that of restoring the dunes, which are disappearing due to the ubiquitous presence of invasive grasses. In the early 1900s, European beach grass was imported and planted on dunes near the mouths of rivers to keep the shifting sand from clogging rivers and obstructing navigation. Dune stabilization was also undertaken to keep sand off the highway. Ultimately, the cure has proven worse than the disease.

Other plants were also introduced, which in combination with the fast-spreading grass, resulted in the spread of vegetation far beyond the original planting sites, drastically altering natural dune processes and the landscape. Aerial photographs taken in 1939 show vegetation over 20 percent of the sand dunes, and photographs of the same region taken in 1989 reveal vegetation covering 80 percent of the sand dunes, essentially choking them and preventing sand from moving and redistributing itself in a natural process.

Other unanticipated impacts of dune stabilization efforts include loss of habitat for native species of plants and animals, such as the western snowy plover, and an increased possibility of wildfire in the dunes.

Unfortunately, the grasses are very difficult to eradicate, as their root systems can extend thirty feet or more. Efforts are underway to test approaches for removing the grasses, including mechanically scraping the foredunes, applying approved herbicides, and setting prescribed fires. The Oregon National Guard has participated in these experimental efforts, as have local volunteer groups.

Along with other federal and state agencies, the Siuslaw National Forest is also actively engaged in protection of the western snowy plover, which lives on sandy beaches and is listed as a threatened species. During its

Men plant dune grasses as part of a Civilian Conservation Corps project, 1936. (Photo courtesy of Suislaw National Forest)

breeding season, between March 15 and September 15, identified nesting sites in dry-sand areas are roped off to the public. Dogs and bicycles are also not allowed on the beaches in these areas, and kite flying is prohibited, as the birds perceive kites as predators. Of the eight nesting sites in Oregon, five occur in the Siuslaw National Forest and the Oregon Dunes National Recreation Area.

In addition, the Siuslaw National Forest is also charged with making a wide variety of recreational activities available to the public, ranging from hiking, birding, fishing, camping, boating, and recreational vehicle use. Another challenge within the Oregon Dunes, then, is that of managing various recreational uses, which at times conflict with each other. The dunes are very popular with users of off-highway vehicles (OHVs); however, the noise and activity associated with their use may be considered intrusive to hikers, birders, or others preferring a more serene experience. Forest Service staff estimates that, of the 1.2 to 1.9 million annual visitors to the Siuslaw National Forest, 25 to 30 percent participate in OHV recreation. It is the most popular activity for those visiting the dunes, and about half of the 32,402 acres in the Oregon Dunes National Recreation Area is available for OHV use.

Some forty years later, a Youth Conservation Corps crew pulls out the dune grass. (Photo courtesy of Siuslaw National Forest)

Although there are designated routes for OHV use, not all OHV riders stay on legal trails, which has resulted in many miles of non-designated, user-created trails. After years of minimal enforcement of this illegal use, the Forest Service is now proposing to formally open some of those trails and to better enforce closure of others.

While walking the four days in and through the dunes, you are most likely to encounter OHVs on the beach between the Florence south jetty (south of parking area 1) and the Siltcoos River, within the dunes but not on the beach south of Winchester Bay, and on the beach north of Horsfall Beach.

DAY 21

Siuslaw River South Jetty
to Oregon Dunes Day Use Area

Distance: 13 miles

Terrain: Beach, trail

Begin: Siuslaw River South Jetty Parking Area

Directions: From US Highway 101, just south of the Siuslaw River Bridge, between mileposts 191 and 192, turn west onto S Jetty Road, which becomes Sand Dunes Road, and follow the signs to the South Jetty Dunes and Beach. Follow Sand Dunes Road as it veers to the right until you have gone a total of 6 miles since turning off the highway to the far end of the park, at parking area 7. Daily recreation fee, applicable federal recreation pass, or Oregon Pacific Coast Passport required.

End: Oregon Dunes Day Use Area

Directions: Turn west off US Highway 101 at the brown Oregon Dunes Day Use Area sign, between mileposts 200 and 201. Daily recreation fee, applicable federal recreation pass, or Oregon Pacific Coast Passport required.

Overview

Day 21 kicks off four consecutive hikes through the Oregon Dunes, all part of the Oregon Dunes National Recreation Area, which is managed by the US Forest Service. These are long hikes and, once you've begun them, there are no opportunities for water, food, or shelter, so it is important to plan accordingly. All four days consist of beach walks and crossing through the dunes themselves, which is in and of itself a challenge because the sand is deep and soft. These four days are also among the most amazing hikes of the entire journey for their unworldly beauty and solitude, especially when you traverse the dunes. Hikers are likely to encounter few, if any, people on these remote stretches of beach, though the serenity may be interrupted by the presence or sounds of OHVs, which are allowed in some parts of the ODNRA.

To shorten this hike, begin farther south—numerous parking areas provide direct access to the beach. Beginning at Parking Area 1 rather than Parking Area 7 eliminates 4 miles.

This route is suggested in lieu of walking through Florence from the north jetty because that option is not particularly scenic and would include some distance on the highway. But those wanting to walk the 8 miles between the north and south jetties would walk 1 mile out N Jetty Road to where it intersects with Rhododendron Drive, turn right, and follow it for 4 miles until reaching US Highway 101 just before it crosses the Siuslaw River Bridge. Rhododendron Drive does not always have a good shoulder for walking. Once getting on US Highway 101, it is then another mile across the bridge and along the highway to reach S Jetty Road. Turn west and follow that road (which becomes Sand Dunes Road) for 2 miles until reaching the beach.

Description

Begin at Parking Area 7 at the northern end of the Siuslaw River south jetty, directly across the water from where Day 20 ended on the north jetty—as if taking a boat, which unfortunately is not doable. Cross the parking area a short distance through the foredunes to the beach. The first 4 miles are within Jetty Park in Florence, where no OHVs are allowed; for the next 5 miles, to the Siltcoos River, the beach is shared with OHVs. After that, they are not allowed again.

Wade the Siltcoos River, which is about 9.5 miles into the hike and which ideally should be timed to be reached at lower tides, and continue on the beach.

At about 12 miles, look carefully on the ridge of the dunes to see a brown post with a faded blue band peeking through the dunes—that indicates the trail to the day-use area, but it's easy to miss. While there is another trail access about 1.5 miles farther south on the beach, it is longer and, as I found out the hard way, requires hiking 4 miles more than by taking the first trail. GPS coordinates for exiting the beach to Oregon Dunes Day Use Area: N 43°50.189', W 124°09.840'.

Follow the trail posts, which take you through shady wooded areas and across the dunes, 1 mile along the Oregon Dunes Trail to Oregon Dunes Day Use Area, which is well worth exploring for its observation platforms and interpretive information about the dunes.

Days 21 and 22: Siuslaw River South Jetty to Winchester Bay

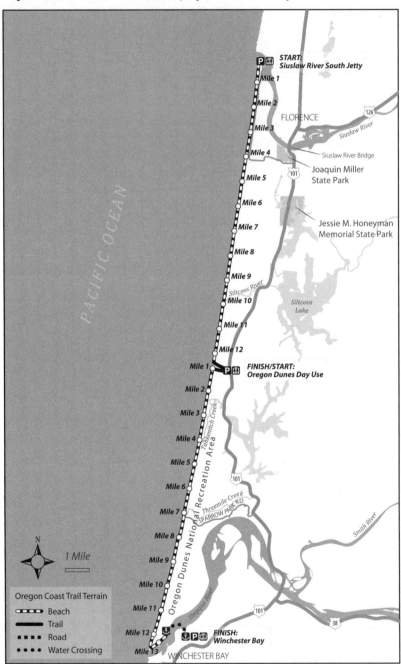

DAY 22

Oregon Dunes Day Use Area to Winchester Bay (with boat ride) OR Oregon Dunes Day Use Area to Sparrow Park Road (without boat ride)

Distance: 13.7 miles with boat ride, 7.2 miles without boat ride

Terrain: Trail, beach; boat ride optional

Begin: Oregon Dunes Day Use Area

Directions: Turn west off US Highway 101 at the brown Oregon Dunes Day Use Area sign, between mileposts 200 and 201. Daily recreation fee, applicable federal recreation pass, or Oregon Pacific Coast Passport required.

End: Winchester Bay with boat ride; Sparrow Park Road without boat ride.

Directions: If taking a boat to Winchester Bay: Turn west off US Highway 101 between mileposts 215 and 216 at Winchester Bay and onto 8th Street. Follow the signs to Salmon Harbor Recreation Area, where there is ample parking.

Without a boat ride, ending at Sparrow Park Road: Turn west off US Highway 101 at milepost 207 onto Sparrow Park Road. Drive 4 miles to the end of the road, where there is limited parking.

Overview

This day begins by hiking through the dunes along the well-marked Oregon Dunes Trail that begins at the Oregon Dunes Day Use Area, where the previous hike ended. Once through the dunes, it's another long stretch of beach walking to the Umpqua River jetty. A boat ride can be prearranged into Winchester Bay (see page 19 for contact information) to avoid considerable highway walking; however, it is very important to carefully plan to be at the designated pickup point at the agreed-upon time.

Walking through the Oregon Dunes provides a surreal hiking experience. (Photo by Greg Lee)

This is a western snowy plover protection area, so during nesting season the dry sands will be roped off and restrictions will be in place for bringing dogs or using bicycles.

Description

Begin by taking the lower trail from the trailhead located in the northwest corner of the parking area next to the restrooms. Follow this pleasant path a mile as it meanders through salal, blackberry, huckleberry, rhododendron, and other indigenous vegetation until it intersects with the beach. Head south on the beach, wading Tahkenitch Creek shortly after mile 4. OHVs are not allowed until Tahkenitch Creek, and then are allowed south of there to the end of the spit. At mile 7, the course diverges depending on if you are taking a boat into Winchester Bay or not.

Option 1—Boat Ride: If taking a boat ride into Winchester Bay, which is highly recommended, continue walking along the beach. Prepare to wade again, this time at Threemile Creek at 7.5 miles. Continue walking along the shoreline for another 5 miles until reaching the jetty.

Walk another mile to reach a sandy cove where a boat can pick you up. To get to the cove, first look for a sandy draw between clumps of vegetation just to the east of the jetty. The draw climbs slightly over a small dune to reveal an obvious sandy trail that is not visible from the beach. Follow it as far as you can, and then walk along the riverside to the left of the jetty until the rocks end. Continue walking to a small sandy cove where the boat will pick you up.

Option 2—No Boat Ride: If a boat ride is not arranged, hikers will need to exit the beach at Sparrow Park Road at mile 7.1, where there is a small parking area.

• •

My attempts at capturing the magnitude and striking characteristics of the Oregon dunes with a camera have ended in a blur of white sand and an utter lack of definition. While it is said that a picture is worth a thousand words, there are times when words can better evoke a mood.

Oregon Dunes
Here, there's a great urge to run,
because there's nowhere to get to.

There's a great urge to lie down,
because everything is like everything else.

Scrub brush grows from nothing,
something crashes off in the distance.
Blue sky and white everywhere.

When you stop on the ridgeline,
it moves you, crumbles
under your bare feet, lowers you deeper.

Here, the easy association is the ocean—
waves over your head, swells for miles.

The harder one is your life—
waves over your head, the lack of horizon.

—Sid Miller

• •

DAY 23

Winchester Bay
to John Dellenback Dunes Trailhead

Distance: 9.5 miles

Terrain: Road, beach, trail

Begin: Winchester Bay

Directions: Turn west off US Highway 101 between mileposts 215 and 216 at Winchester Bay and onto 8th Street. Follow the signs to Salmon Harbor Recreation Area, where there is ample parking.

End: John Dellenback Dunes Trailhead

Directions: Turn west off US Highway 101 at the sign indicating the John Dellenback Dunes Trailhead, located between mileposts 222 and 223. Parking is available. Daily recreation fee, applicable federal recreation pass, or Oregon Pacific Coast Passport required.

Overview

Day 23 continues dune hiking. It begins in the fishing village of Winchester Bay and heads south along the beach until the John Dellenback Dunes Trail (formerly referred to as the Umpqua Dunes Trail and may still be signed as such), which leads you through the dunes for over 2 miles to the John Dellenback Dunes Trailhead parking area. The John Dellenback Dunes Trail is extraordinarily beautiful and offers a unique hiking experience by traversing the heart of the dunes.

Description

This hike can be started anywhere along the marina in Winchester Bay. Head south and turn right at the stop sign to follow Salmon Harbor Drive west and south as it curves through Windy Cove Park. In summer, the park is sure to be filled with RVs, campers, and tents cheek by jowl. Continue along the road next to a small sheltered cove and turn onto an unmarked gravel road that heads south. Follow it to nearly the end and take one of several sandy paths that lead over small foredunes onto the beach, just south of the Triangle oyster beds, where fresh oysters are farmed.

At this point, you will be 2.5 miles into the hike, assuming it started in the middle of the marina area. Walk along the beach for another 4.5 miles and look carefully along the vegetation line for a nondescript, brown trail sign indicating Umpqua Dunes Trail (the sign may have been corrected to read John Dellenback Dunes Trail by now but was not when I was there). While it's an obvious trail that leads through the foredunes with tall grass, it is not immediately visible from the beach, so be looking for it.

Enter a forested area and walk about 0.5 mile until it opens up onto a most amazing sight of towering white sand dunes that makes one feel transported to another continent, if not another planet.

• •

This is the stuff of science fiction and, as a matter of fact, this very landscape inspired Frank Herbert to write the well-known novel *Dune* in 1965, as he told one interviewer:

> The idea came from an article (I was going to do an article, which I never did) about the control of sand dunes. What many people don't realize is that the United States has pioneered in this, how to control the flow of sand dunes, and it started up here at Florence, Oregon.... Sand dunes are like waves in a large body of water; they just are slower. And the people treating them as fluid learn to control them.... Fluid mechanics, with sand. And the whole idea fascinated me, so I started researching sand dunes and of course from sand dunes it's a logical idea to go into a desert.

• •

Although referred to as a trail, the route through the dunes is not a linear or logical path because the large, open mounds of sand are constantly moving and changing shapes. Look for the brown posts and keep the large tree island to the right. At the end of the tree island, occasional trail markers provide

Winchester Bay is known for its oysters.

guidance. Walk through the dunes however possible, heading east for about 1.5 miles through the dunes until coming upon a well-established trail. Upon reaching a fork in the trail—left to Eel Creek Campground, right to Dellenback Trail—go to the right and follow the trail 0.5 mile to the parking lot.

Days 23 and 24: Winchester Bay to to Horsfall Beach

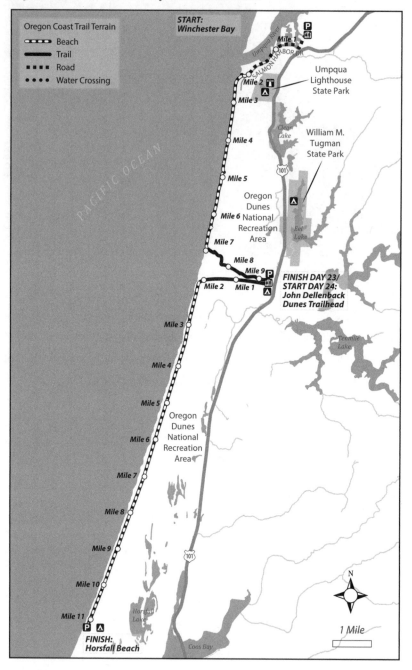

DAY 24

John Dellenback Dunes Trailhead to Horsfall Beach

Distance: 11.5 miles

Terrain: Trail, beach

Begin: John Dellenback Dunes Trailhead

Directions: Turn west from US Highway 101 at the sign indicating access to the John Dellenback Dunes Trailhead, located between mileposts 222 and 223. Parking is available. Daily recreation fee, applicable federal recreation pass, or Oregon Pacific Coast Passport required.

End: Horsfall Beach

Directions: From US Highway 101, between mileposts 233 and 234 and immediately south of the McCullough Memorial Bridge in Coos Bay, turn west onto Trans Pacific Lane. Follow it about a mile to Horsfall Beach Road; take that road about 3.5 miles to the parking area. Daily recreation fee, applicable federal recreation pass, or Oregon Pacific Coast Passport required.

Overview

This is the final hike through the dunes. You will retrace your steps until reaching the beach, and it is all walking on sand from there.

Description

Start at the John Dellenback Dunes Trailhead and walk the trail for about 2.2 miles back through the dunes to the beach. Continue south for an uninterrupted beach walk for about 9 miles to Horsfall Beach. Horsfall

Using ATVs is the most popular activity within the Oregon Dunes National Recreation Area. (Photo courtesy of Siuslaw National Forest)

Beach is a major staging area for OHVs, so you will probably see and hear them as you approach it.

The egress off the beach may be difficult to spot. Look for a wooden platform overlooking the beach just past a sign prohibiting motorized vehicles; head for it and hike through the foredunes to the parking lot, which is not visible from the beach. GPS coordinates for exiting the beach at Horsfall Beach: N 43°27.240', W 124°16.661'.

DAY 25

Horsfall Beach to Ferry Road Park

Distance: 5.5 miles

Terrain: Road, highway

Begin: Horsfall Beach

Directions: From US Highway 101, between mileposts 233 and 234 and immediately south of the McCullough Memorial Bridge in Coos Bay, turn west onto Trans Pacific Lane. Follow it about a mile to Horsfall Beach Road; take that road 3.5 miles to the parking area. Daily recreation fee, applicable federal recreation pass, or Oregon Pacific Coast Passport required.

End: Ferry Road Park

Directions: From Highway 101, between mileposts 234 and 235, immediately south of the McCullough Memorial Bridge in North Bend, turn east onto Ferry Road and continue 0.2 mile to the paved parking area on the left.

Overview

This day consists entirely of road walking and primarily serves as a link to connect the beach north of Coos Bay with Ferry Road Park in North Bend, where the Sawmill & Tribal Trail begins on Day 25. While very little walking on this day requires hugging the highway shoulder, you should nonetheless be attentive of traffic. A highlight includes the opportunity to walk across the bridge named posthumously for Conde McCullough. This bridge is considered one of his greatest achievements.

The Coos Bay (McCullough Memorial) Bridge under construction in 1935 looked like a roller coaster. (Photo courtesy of ODOT, Bridge Engineering Section)

Description

Unfortunately, no trail exists through the Horsfall Beach day-use and campground areas, so from the parking area, follow Horsfall Beach Road out of the park for 2.5 miles. This is not a busy road, but neither does it always provide for a comfortable place to walk. Upon reaching the intersection, turn left to walk a scenic mile along the TransPacific Parkway, a causeway over Coos Bay, to the intersection with US Highway 101. Walk the highway shoulder 0.7 mile—some of it plenty wide and some of it providing only a narrow passage—to the pedestrian access of the McCullough Memorial Bridge.

Walk 1 mile over the bridge and descend the elegant, curved stairway at the south end. Walk under the bridge and follow a paved path that curves to the right. Shortly, three paths converge; take the middle path for 0.2 mile and cut across the playground to reach the parking area.

DAY 26

Ferry Road Park to Charleston

Distance: 10.9 miles

Terrain: Road, trail

Begin: Ferry Road Park

Directions: From Highway 101, between mileposts 234 and 235, immediately south of the McCullough Memorial Bridge in North Bend, turn east onto Ferry Road and continue 0.2 mile to the paved parking area on the left.

End: Charleston

Directions: From US Highway 101, between mileposts 235 and 236, turn west onto Virginia Avenue, which becomes Highway 540. Follow the signs to Charleston and Ocean Beaches. At Charleston, turn right onto Boat Basin Road, which leads to the marina. Public parking is available in the marina.

Coos Transit provides service between Charleston and North Bend (transfer required).

Overview

This hike incorporates the Sawmill & Tribal Trail, which is recommended as an interesting deviation from the official OCT that does not add any distance. Completed in 2011, this urban trail is the result of a collaborative effort and various partnerships, including the Cities of Coos Bay and North Bend; the Confederated Tribes of Coos, Lower Umpqua, and Siuslaw Indians; the Coos Historical & Maritime Museum; the Community Coalition of Empire; South Coast Striders; and the National Coast Trail Association.

It follows paths developed by Coos tribal ancestors that connected their bayside villages and hunting grounds. Later, settlers also used these trails. Along the route, walkers learn about local history from informational displays located at some of the thirty-five wooden posts that mark the route. A free brochure—available at local visitor information centers—includes a detailed map of the route as well as explanations of the points of interest along the way, and it is very helpful to have one.

Oregon's Merci Boxcar is displayed in front of the Coos Historical & Maritime Museum.

Merci boxcars, which once transported soldiers and horses during World War I, were filled with gifts and given to every American state by the French people after World War II as an expression of gratitude to their allies.

The day's walk concludes with 5 miles of walking local roads into Charleston. Those wanting to shorten the hike or eliminate road walking could conclude at the Empire docks.

Description

The Sawmill & Tribal Trail starts at the foot of Ferry Road Park in North Bend. From the parking lot, walk to the water and turn right to find the first cedar post, which stands at the former site of Asa

Day 26: Ferry Road Park to Charleston

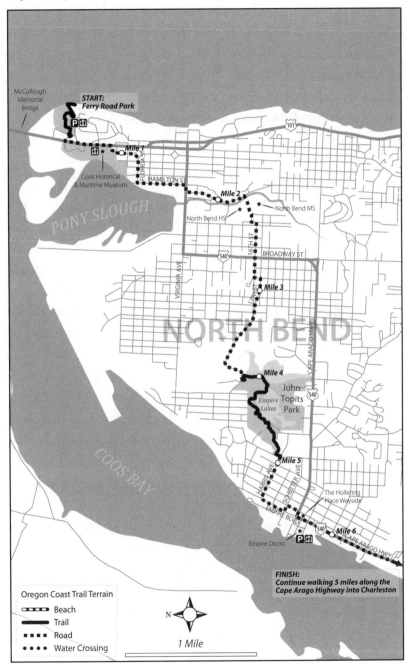

Simpson's sawmill and shipyard. Post 2 is situated where ferry service once linked North Bend and Glasgow. From here, retrace steps along the pathway back to the park. The trail goes past a baseball field on the right and then veers left and under the McCullough Memorial Bridge. On the other side of the bridge, walk along a little trail and the sidewalk next to US Highway 101 to the Coos Historical & Maritime Museum, which displays Oregon's Merci Boxcar in front of the building, and then through another small park that once was the site of a local baseball field.

Exit the park onto Union Avenue, walk a couple of blocks, and turn right onto Florida Street and then left onto Hamilton Street. Upon reaching Virginia Avenue, turn right, and in one block get onto Harrison Street. Continue a few blocks until reaching a pedestrian bridge to the right. Cross it and walk between the North Bend middle and high schools, and onto 16th Street. Continue along 16th Street a few blocks and walk up the hill until reaching Madrona. Turn left, and in one block, turn right at 17th Street. This street becomes Lakeshore Drive (also referred to as Old Stage Road). Shortly after the lakes come into view, enter John Topits Park and make a sharp left turn (there are three divergent paths) to follow the path down (south). This part of the trail is somewhat confusing because of a separate set of posts. All of the informational posts in the park relate to the natural flora and how plants were used by local Native American tribes. Follow the path near Lower Lake in a counterclockwise direction. (Do not cross the path with lakes on both sides of it.)

Near the parking area between posts 22 and 23, make a sharp right down the hill and follow the path west out of the park. Upon reaching the road, turn left and then right onto Harris Avenue. Walk along this unpaved road until it ends at the mud flats at N Empire Boulevard. Turn left, and in two blocks, turn left on Schetter Avenue, right on N Marple Street, right on Cape Arago Highway (Newmark Avenue), and left on S Mill Street to find the last few informational posts of the Sawmill & Tribal Trail in close proximity to each other. Post 34 is located at the Hollering Place.

The Hollering Place is a site of special significance to coastal Indian tribes. The Hanis Coos Tribe had established numerous villages along the bay and in surrounding areas, including one called El-ka-titc, now known as the Hollering Place, in what is the present-day Empire District of Coos Bay.

Located on the shore of a major beach trail across the bay from the sand spit, where the lower bay is narrow, people would holler over to the villages for someone to pick them up in their canoes, a practice which continued when trappers and early settlers arrived with their families—hence its name. The first permanent white settlement in the area, Empire City, was established there in 1853, claiming land that Indians had lived on for many generations.

Presently, there are plans to redevelop the area. These efforts will be overseen by the Confederated Tribes of Coos, Lower Umpqua, and Siuslaw Indians. They intend to build a high-end hotel, cottages, a restaurant, a retail plaza, and a promenade.

From the wayside, it's just over 5 miles of road walking along Cape Arago Highway into Charleston. Upon leaving the docks area, turn right onto Empire Boulevard and walk 4.5 miles. Some of the road has a good shoulder, and some segments on the east side of the road have intermittent sidewalk or a bike path. Other parts of the road, unfortunately, do not provide good pedestrian amenities, so take care. Cross the bridge over South Slough and turn right onto Boat Basin Road and right again onto Kingfisher Drive to reach the Charleston Marina.

DAY 27

Charleston to Cape Arago State Park

Distance: 7.5 miles

Terrain: Road, beach, trail

Begin: Charleston

Directions: From US Highway 101, between mileposts 235 and 236, turn west onto Virginia Avenue, which becomes Highway 540. Follow the signs to Charleston and Ocean Beaches. At Charleston, turn right onto Boat Basin Road, which leads to the marina. Public parking is available in the marina.

End: Cape Arago State Park

Directions: Follow directions above to Charleston. Instead of turning onto Boat Basin Road, continue on Cape Arago Highway 5.5 miles until it ends at the parking area for Cape Arago State Park.

Overview

This hike begins in the sleepy fishing village of Charleston. It then continues a mile on Bastendorff Beach and through the heart of three jewels of Oregon State Parks—Sunset Bay, Shore Acres, and Cape Arago. The walk provides spectacular scenery along a cliffside, a chance to enjoy the formal gardens at Shore Acres—where something is always in bloom—and opportunities for sea lion and whale sightings. This hike offers diverse terrain and is among the most beautiful along the OCT. Unfortunately it is poorly signed and, given the proliferation of trails within and between the three parks, it is easy to get confused.

The crabbing is excellent in Charleston.

Description

Begin by walking through the Charleston Marina on Guano Rock Lane until reaching Boat Basin Road, where you turn right, then immediately left onto Coos Head Road. Go uphill about 0.5 mile, and at the fork in the road, turn left onto Chicken Loop Road (no road sign). Turn right again back onto Coos Head Road and go 0.3 mile to get onto Bastendorff Beach. This marks 1.6 miles into the hike.

Walk 1 mile on the beach, which ends just south of Yoakam Point. Look for a narrow sandy path heading east and at the base of the cliff. The trail is at the edge of park territory but is directly adjacent to a private RV and tent camp. Walk a short distance on the path until reaching a rough but defined trail leading up the cliff. Take this trail through the woods 0.25 mile, staying to the left to avoid spurs to the right. Upon reaching Cape Arago Highway, turn right and walk a dozen yards or so along the side of the road. Cross the highway to find a trail slightly sunken below the road, the Bastendorff Bog Trail, which may be hard to spot. It leads through the woods on a level trail to the hiker-biker camp at Sunset Bay State Park in 1.25 miles. GPS coordinates for beginning of Bastendorff Bog Trail: N 43°20.379', W 124°21.622'.

Day 27: Charleston to Cape Arago State Park

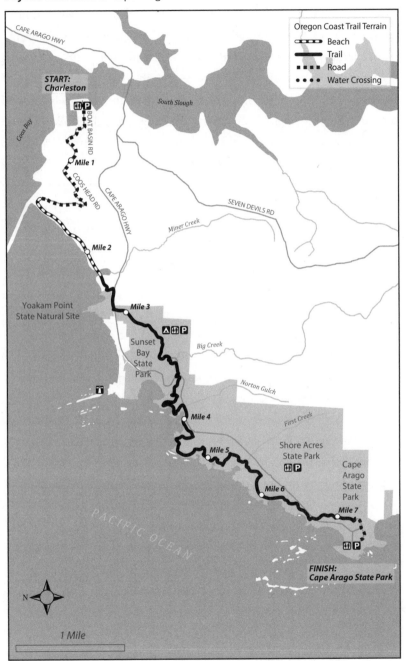

Exit the campground at the ranger station. Turn right and, just before reaching the road, take the signed Beach Access Trail, which tunnels under the road, loops through a picnic area, and crosses a small bridge. Turn left and, just beyond the restrooms, cross another bridge to take the trail through the woods until it intersects with a path heading uphill to the left. At the top of the hill, follow the trail counterclockwise around a group camping area. Once leaving the camp area, the trail opens up to dramatic views and vistas, including a glimpse of the Cape Arago Lighthouse in the distance.

••

The Cape Arago Lighthouse is situated on a small island 2.5 miles from Cape Arago, and is visible from the Oregon Coast Trail between Sunset Bay State Park and Shore Acres State Park, and from Bastendorff Beach County Park. An original structure was built in 1866, and the current lighthouse was built in 1934. The island, originally called Chief's Island, was inhabited by Coos Indians prior to white settlement. Because their ancestors had lived and were buried there, the Coos Indians continued to have a strong connection to the island and the nearby mainland, despite its long use as a lighthouse station.

Following the drowning of Coos tribesman Henry M. Brainard near the lighthouse in 1948, his widow sought permission to place a marker on the station grounds, a request that the US Coast Guard denied for years. Ultimately, through an act of Congress sponsored by Oregon Senator Wayne Morse, the marker was placed.

In 2008, federal legislation allowed the transfer of Cape Arago Lighthouse from the US Coast Guard to the Confederated Tribes of Coos, Lower Umpqua, and Siuslaw Indians. According to the legislation, the tribes must make the station available to the general public for educational, park, recreational, cultural, or historic preservation purposes. In 2013, the transfer was completed in a ceremony including all parties, returning historically and traditionally important lands to the tribes.

••

Upon reaching the road, turn right and walk a short distance inside the guardrail; then turn inland onto another trail (it can be frustrating that most trails are not named or signed within these parks) after about 0.2 mile. Shortly after 1 mile, you will reach a juncture; either the path straight ahead or the one to the right will lead into Shore Acres State Park, but taking the one on the right provides a slightly longer and considerably more scenic route—scenic because it skirts a cliffside affording incredible views of an escarpment carved by centuries of exposure to the natural elements. From this incredible vantage point, you will enjoy glimpses of pocket beaches and coves, of cinnamon-colored, striped rock formations, of trees barely clinging to the hillsides, and possibly of sea lions basking on the flat rocks below.

At the next intersection, take the trail to the right, which heads downhill, down some stairs, and up again, eventually becoming a paved path leading to the observation building with interpretive information explaining the origins of Shore Acres State Park.

• •

The lumber entrepreneur Asa Meade Simpson started the area's first shipyard in North Bend in the late 1850s, and he remained active in the business until his death at age ninety. The site of the Simpson sawmill is visited as part of the Sawmill & Tribal Trail on Day 26. His eldest son, Louis J. Simpson, carried on the family business and founded the community of North Bend. He was also an aspiring politician—in 1918 he unsuccessfully ran for governor.

In 1906, Louis Simpson gave his wife a Christmas gift of a summer home they called Shore Acres. Over time, the estate developed into an elaborate mansion with a heated indoor swimming pool and other luxuries. The grounds also included five acres of formal gardens that were tended to by twelve full-time gardeners. Trees, shrubs, and plants were imported from around the world. The mansion burned in 1921, but work began on a new mansion in 1927. With the onset of the Great Depression, work stopped, and the Simpsons moved out in 1936. They sold the property to the State of Oregon for $29,000 in 1942. The mansion was used briefly as barracks in World War II and was torn down in 1948.

The gardens are still the centerpiece of the park. The plantings at Shore Acres have been designed to take advantage of the area's mild climate, with different kinds of flowers or trees blooming all seasons of the year.

· ·

From here, follow the paved path to the left to go to the gardens. Walk through the manicured formal gardens and exit through a gate to the right of the lily pond.

Turn left on the trail to Simpson Beach, a beautiful and secluded cove, and at the intersection reached in 0.3 mile, turn right onto a lovely bark-dust trail fringed with salal and ferns follow it until you reach another intersection. This is about 6.5 miles into the hike. Turn right—the trail loops below the road and comes to another intersection. Turn right again and walk until you reach Simpson Reef/Shell Island Overlook, a great place to see California sea lions, Steller sea lions, harbor seals, and elephant seals. Walk through the overlook area (there may be volunteers with telescopes or binoculars, so take the time to have a peek), cross the road, and take the trail that leads straight up the hillside. When reaching a junction after 0.5 mile, take a right turn and then a quick left turn onto a service road that leads into the Cape Arago State Park parking area.

DAY 28

South Slough National Estuarine Research Reserve to Seven Devils State Recreation Site

Distance: 7.1 miles

Terrain: Road

Begin: South Slough National Estuarine Research Reserve

Directions: From the north: Turn west from US Highway 101, between mileposts 235 and 236, onto Virginia Avenue, which becomes Highway 540. Follow the signs to Charleston and Ocean Beaches. After crossing the bridge over South Slough at Charleston, continue straight on the Cape Arago Highway and turn left onto Seven Devils Road. Follow it 4 miles and turn left into the reserve, where parking and restrooms are available.

    From the south: Turn left from US Highway 101, between mileposts 252 and 253, onto West Beaver Hill Road at the sign indicating South Slough Reserve, Charleston, and Ocean Beaches. Take it about 9 miles to reach the entrance of the preserve on the right. Parking and restrooms are available.

End: Seven Devils State Recreation Site

Directions: From US Highway 101, between mile markers 257 and 258, turn west onto Seven Devils Road. Drive 4.5 miles on this road and turn left into the wayside and parking area.

Overview

Currently, there is no walking link from Cape Arago back to the beach and on to Seven Devils State Recreation Site. Options for crossing over Cape Arago, such as walking through privately owned timberlands, are

Walking along Seven Devils Road is the only way to get between Cape Arago State Park and Seven Devils State Recreation Site.

being explored but have not yet reached fruition and are therefore not yet viable, or at least official, solutions. Officially, the OCT has hikers back-tracking from Cape Arago to Seven Devils Road and walking that road to Seven Devils State Recreation Site. While purists may wish to follow this route, I suggest an alternative that will cover most of the official trail while eliminating the most difficult stretch of it.

The walk consists of 7.1 miles of up-and-down road walking along Seven Devils Road—some of it pleasant, some of it not. But it is an opportunity to walk a remote and scenic coastal road and is a nice change of pace from the beach.

Description

Begin at the South Slough National Estuarine Research Reserve, which is a lovely and interesting place to explore. Starting here eliminates the first 4 miles of walking on Seven Devils Road, which offers very little if any shoulder and abounds with blind curves.

• •

The 4,800-acre South Slough National Estuarine Research Reserve encompasses a mixture of open-water channels, tidal and freshwater wetlands, riparian areas, and forested uplands. It was designated in

1974 as the first unit of the National Estuarine Research Reserve System, which is a network of estuarine habitats protected and managed for the purposes of long-term research and education. The estuary houses an interpretive center and offers a network of both land and water trails for exploring the area.

....

After 3 miles, the road intersects with West Beaver Hill Road. Continue straight to stay on Seven Devils Road, which transitions to a gravel road, heading steeply downhill. It goes up and down again. Here, the road is scenic and a little desolate, with few houses or developments of any kind. Shortly after the road becomes paved again, turn right at the sign to the wayside that is Seven Devils State Recreation Site.

DAY 29

Seven Devils State Recreation Site to Bullards Beach State Park

Distance: 5.5 miles or 8.1 miles on high-tide route
Terrain: Beach/Beach and trail on high-tide route
Begin: Seven Devils State Recreation Site
Directions: From US Highway 101, between mile markers 257 and 258, turn west onto Seven Devils Road. Drive 4.5 miles on this road and turn left into the wayside and parking area.
End: Bullards Beach State Park
Directions: From US Highway 101, turn west into Bullards Beach State Park between mileposts 259 and 260, just north of the Bullards Bridge. Follow signs to beach parking area.

Overview

This hike is tide dependent because Fivemile Point, reached at 1.25 miles into the hike, must be rounded at or near low tide. Fortunately, a high-tide alternative also allows for a satisfying hike, although it adds about 3 miles to the total distance. For either the high-tide or the low-tide option, this hike can be extended by walking the full length of the beach—another 1.5 miles—and ending at the Coquille River Lighthouse, which is open to the public, and where there is also parking.

Description

Option 1—Low or lower tides: At lower tides, begin the hike by dropping down to the beach from the wayside to cross a small creek. Head south, walking on the beach for 1.25 miles, and round Fivemile Point. Then it is a straight shot of just over 4 miles on the beach.

Option 2—High tide: If it is not possible to round Fivemile Point because the tide is too high, or if a longer and more diverse hike is preferred, the alternative route is also very pleasant.

As with Option 1, begin at the wayside and head south on the beach. At 0.6 mile, look for a trail sign at the edge of the beach leading up a path. The trail heads up steeply for a short distance, then levels out to provide panoramic views of the beach below. It travels along a grassy path, at times along an easement between two fences bordering private property. At 1.3 miles, you will reach a gate; walk around it and look for Oregon Coast Trail signs. This trail is very well marked, probably to avoid the possibility of trespassing on private property. Continue the zigzag trail until it hits Whiskey Run Road after 2.6 miles. Turn right and walk 0.9 mile until reaching the beach. Here you are 3.5 miles into the hike if you took the high-tide route.

From Whiskey Run Road, the rest of the hike is a beach walk of about 4.5 miles. The beach borders the Bandon Dunes Golf Resort, but there is otherwise little development. GPS coordinates for exiting the beach at Bullards Beach State Park: N 43°08.745', W 124°25.008'.

Day 29: Seven Devils State Recreation Site to Bullards Beach State Park

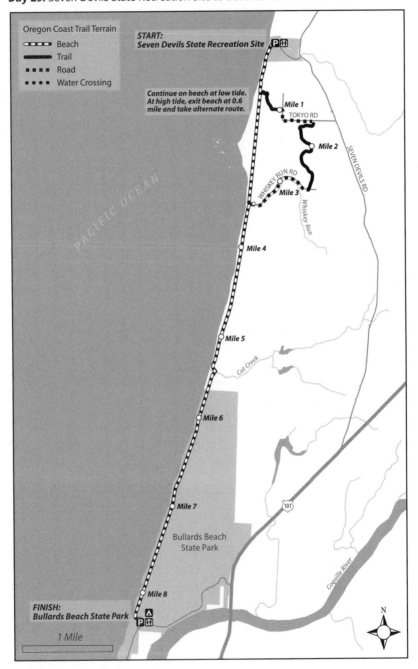

DAY 30

Bullards Beach State Park to China Creek

Distance: 8.7 miles

Terrain: Trail, highway, road, beach

Begin: Bullards Beach State Park

Directions: From US Highway 101, turn west into Bullards Beach State Park between mileposts 259 and 260, just north of the Bullards Bridge. Follow signs to beach parking area.

End: China Creek

Directions: From US Highway 101, turn west on Beach Loop Drive between mileposts 277 and 278. Follow it 1 mile and turn at the sign for China Creek. A small parking area and restrooms are available at the wayside.

Overview

The hike begins at Bullards Beach State Park, travels through the town of Bandon, and concludes with walking 3.5 miles along one of the most picturesque stretches of beach on the entire coastline. At the end of this day, you'll want to put your feet up, pour a glass of fine Oregon Pinot noir, and make a toast to the legacies of Oswald West and Tom McCall.

Description

Begin the hike at the beach access parking area of Bullards Beach State Park. Pick up a paved path directly east of the parking lot and follow it through the park, parallel to the main road. After 1 mile, the path reaches the campground; here, cross the main road and walk along a grassy pathway next to it to reach the park exit at 1.35 miles. Walk a short distance along the shoulder of US Highway 101 until you come to Bullards Bridge, which spans the Coquille River.

Cross the bridge with extreme care because there is no shoulder and no pedestrian walkway; however, it is not long—0.1 mile. Look for a break in the traffic and scurry across or, as I did, ask a driver leaving the park and heading into Bandon to follow you slowly with lights flashing until you safely cross the bridge. Once across it, veer right onto Riverside Drive NE and then right again onto First Street SE, which takes walkers along Bandon's waterfront and through town. Turn right onto Jetty Road SW, leading to Bandon's South Jetty County Park, reached 5 miles into the hike.

Walk south on the beach. As the sound of the foghorn recedes, the looming shapes of seastacks emerge and hikers pass through a seascape of rock formations and caves gracing the shore like silent muses. Some of the rock islands offshore, which are all protected for nesting birds, have names like Sisters, Table Rock, Face Rock, and Cat and Kittens.

After walking about 3 miles on the beach, you will see where the Bandon State Natural Area begins, as evidenced by the lack of housing or other development along the bluff. Continue another 0.5 mile down the beach, wade China Creek, and head inland alongside the creek until finding the pathway leading in 0.2 mile up to the wayside at China Creek. The path can be easy to miss from the beach. During the summer, the area may be cordoned off due to snowy plover protection, and the signs indicating the protection zones may be a helpful landmark. GPS coordinates for exiting the beach at China Creek: N 43°04.377', W 124°26.114'.

Day 30: Bullards Beach State Park to China Creek

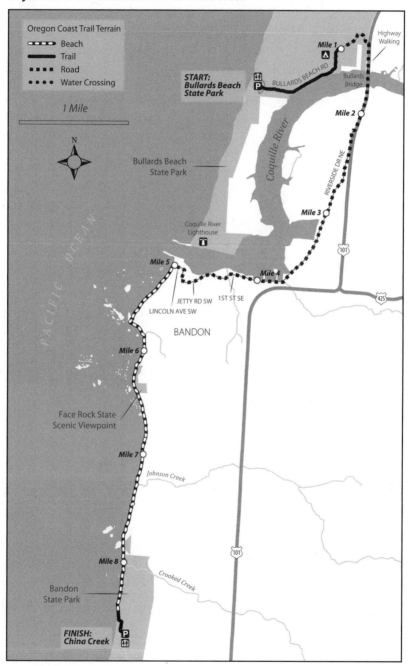

DAYS 31–40

Bandon to California Border

Overview

The final section of the OCT travels along the southern coast, highlighted by trails through Cape Sebastian and the well-named Samuel H. Boardman State Scenic Corridor. Day 31 is one of the most remote beach hikes of the entire journey—it consists of nearly 13 miles on the beach between China Creek and Floras Lake at Boice Cope County Park, with no opportunities to exit the beach in between. From Floras Lake, you will hike over Blacklock Point and conclude with a short walk on the beach, a wade through the Sixes River at low tide, and a climb to the top of Cape Blanco with its picturesque lighthouse. On Day 33, you will resume hiking at Cape Blanco, enter the beach, and cross the Elk River at low tide. Day 34 offers a wonderful variety of terrain by walking through the town of Port Orford, along the beach near Battle Rock Park, and through the fern-laden trails on Humbug Mountain.

The largest gap of the OCT lies between the south end of Humbug Mountain and Ophir. Although this is a very scenic stretch of the coast, I recommend these 11 miles, which would otherwise require primarily walking along the highway, be eliminated. On Day 35 you'll travel along beach and trail and on an old highway as far as the Rogue River north jetty. The trail resumes at the same place on Day 36 and takes you through the town of Gold Beach, along beautiful beaches, and up a challenging trail for 4 miles to the top of Cape Sebastian. You'll start the next day (Day 37) at Cape Sebastian and head downhill to the beach leading to Pistol River—another scenic beach with seastacks and other interesting rock formations.

You will hike two days through the Samuel H. Boardman State Scenic Corridor, and they are among the most magnificent of the entire hike—they are also among the most strenuous because of the many ups and downs. These hikes conclude by entering Harris Beach State Park at the end of Day 39.

The last hike is walked through Brookings, and fittingly the trail ends on sand by accessing the beach at low tide at McVay Rock State Recreation Site, crossing the Winchuck River, and hiking the last mile or so on the beach to the border separating Oregon from California.

You will visit the towns of Bandon, Port Orford, Gold Beach, and Brookings.

Table 6. Days 31–40: Bandon to California Border

Day	Hike	Miles	Terrain	Considerations
31	China Creek to Boice Cope County Park	12.9	Beach	low tide
32	Boice Cope County Park to Cape Blanco SP	7.3	Trail, beach	low tide
33	Cape Blanco SP to Paradise Point SRS	5.6	Trail, beach	low tide
34	Paradise Point SRS to Humbug Mountain SP	9.6	Road, beach, highway, trail	low tide
35	Ophir Wayside SP Rest Area to Rogue River North Jetty	9.9	Beach, trail, road	
36	Rogue River North Jetty to Cape Sebastian SSC	11.4	Road, beach, trail	
37	Cape Sebastian SSC to Pistol River SSV	5.6	Trail, beach	
38	Arch Rock Picnic Area to Whaleshead Beach Picnic Area	8.6	Trail, beach	low tide

Day	Hike	Miles	Terrain	Considerations
39	Whaleshead Beach Viewpoint to Harris Beach SP	7.9	Trail, beach, highway, road	
40	Harris Beach SP to Crissey Field SRS	8.9	Trail, road, beach	low tide

Days 31–40: South Coast Overview

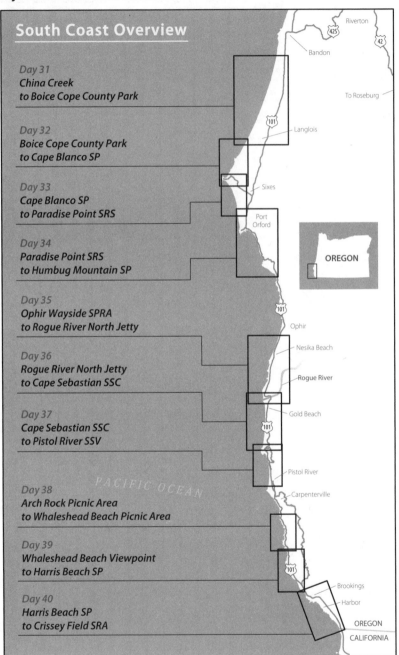

South Coast Overview

Day 31
**China Creek
to Boice Cope County Park**

Day 32
**Boice Cope County Park
to Cape Blanco SP**

Day 33
**Cape Blanco SP
to Paradise Point SRS**

Day 34
**Paradise Point SRS
to Humbug Mountain SP**

Day 35
**Ophir Wayside SPRA
to Rogue River North Jetty**

Day 36
**Rogue River North Jetty
to Cape Sebastian SSC**

Day 37
**Cape Sebastian SSC
to Pistol River SSV**

Day 38
**Arch Rock Picnic Area
to Whaleshead Beach Picnic Area**

Day 39
**Whaleshead Beach Viewpoint
to Harris Beach SP**

Day 40
**Harris Beach SP
to Crissey Field SRA**

Riverton
Bandon
To Roseburg
Langlois
Sixes
Port Orford
OREGON
Ophir
Nesika Beach
Rogue River
Gold Beach
Pistol River
Carpenterville
PACIFIC OCEAN
Brookings
Harbor
OREGON
CALIFORNIA

DAY 31

China Creek to Boice Cope County Park

Distance: 12.9 miles

Terrain: Beach

Begin: China Creek

Directions: From US Highway 101, turn west on Beach Loop Drive between mileposts 277 and 278. Follow the road 1 mile and turn at the sign for China Creek. A small parking area and restrooms are available at the wayside.

End: Boice Cope County Park

Directions: From US Highway 101, turn west between mileposts 289 and 290 onto Floras Lake Loop and turn west onto Floras Lake Road. Follow it to the end, where it veers to the left. Then turn right onto Boice Cope Lane. There is a small parking area where the road ends.

Overview

Today's hike offers miles and miles—and more miles—of a remote beach with no access points in between. For that reason, it is not possible to shorten this hike, and it is important to carry plenty of water and to be prepared for a slog, at times. But, with the exception of the hikes through the Oregon Dunes National Recreation Area, few beach walks along the Oregon Coast are as pristine and unpopulated as this one. Therefore, it offers good beachcombing. It is also important to time the hike to cross the New River at or near low tide, as it is not passable at high tide, even in summer.

Description

From China Creek, take the path at the north end of the small parking lot that leads to the beach, cross a small stream, and head south. Walk along the beach and cross the New River at or near low tide, which is reached 1.75 miles into the hike.

The first 6 miles or so are on firm sand and are fine for walking. After that, however, the beach conditions change and present a challenge. The shore next to the beach slopes, and the sand is so soft that is difficult to walk on. The ground is flatter higher up but is pebbly, coarse, and slow going at times. This is a western snowy plover protection area, and during nesting season, the upper dry sands are roped off. The New River flows behind the dunes but is mainly not visible from the shore until the end of the hike.

This is a good area for beachcombing, as few people come here, so the lucky may find interesting shells, sand dollars, rocks, pieces of driftwood, and the occasional buoy encrusted with barnacles that has washed ashore from who knows where.

At about mile 12.5, start looking for an egress off the beach that leads into Boice Cope County Park adjacent to Floras Lake. During nesting season, there may be signs indicating the plover protection area near the trail, but the actual sandy pathway is easy to miss. GPS coordinates for exiting the beach to Floras Lake: W 43°07.477', N 124°26.709'.

From there, a well-established trail will lead from the beach to the parking area in 0.4 mile.

DAY 32

Boice Cope County Park to
Cape Blanco State Park

Distance: 7.3 miles

Terrain: Trail, beach

Begin: Boice Cope County Park

Directions: From US Highway 101, turn west between mileposts 289 and 290 onto Floras Lake Loop and turn west onto Floras Lake Road. Follow it to the end, where it veers to the left. Then turn right onto Boice Cope Lane. There is a small parking area where the road ends.

End: Cape Blanco State Park

Directions: From US Highway 101, turn west between mileposts 296 and 297 onto Cape Blanco Road and continue 5 miles until reaching the small parking area just before the gated road leading to the lighthouse.

Overview

This is a diverse and lovely hike that travels around Floras Lake, through a wooded path on Blacklock Point, continues a mile on a remote beach, and ends at Cape Blanco Lighthouse. Be aware that the trails over Blacklock Point are not well marked, and it is easy to get confused. It is also important that you time the hike to reach the Sixes River at lower tides.

Description

Start the hike at Floras Lake in Boice Cope County Park, which is calm and serene in early morning and often lively and colorful with wind surfers when the wind picks up.

OCT hikers wade the Sixes River at lower tides as they approach Cape Blanco.

A sandy trail skirts the lake counterclockwise, heading south. After 1 mile, the trail heads up along the edge of the cliffs (do not go onto the beach). Stay straight at the first trail intersection—this will put you on the Airport–Floras Lake Trail—which continues as a fairly level and shady route for 2.25 miles through the forest until it terminates at the end of the Cape Blanco State Airport inactive runway. Cross the field between the tarmac and the shrubbery to find, directly across the field, a brown trail sign indicating a path heading west.

Take the first right turn, and in less than 0.1 mile, turn right again. In another 0.2 mile, find a sign directing hikers to Coastal Trail, Blacklock Point, or Floras Lake. Take the path to the left toward Blacklock Point. Continue for 1 mile, bearing left at junctions where there are signs. When coming to an open campsite area, take the steep path down to the beach. Follow the beach south about 1.25 miles to the Sixes River. Look for the most advantageous place to cross, and wade it at lower tides.

From there, hike 1.5 miles on a remote beach studded with greenish-blue boulders and follow its curve around a small bay. Just before the beach ends, take a sandy path heading straight up the grassy slope, which emerges at the road leading to Cape Blanco Lighthouse.

Day 32: Boice Cope County Park to Cape Blanco State Park

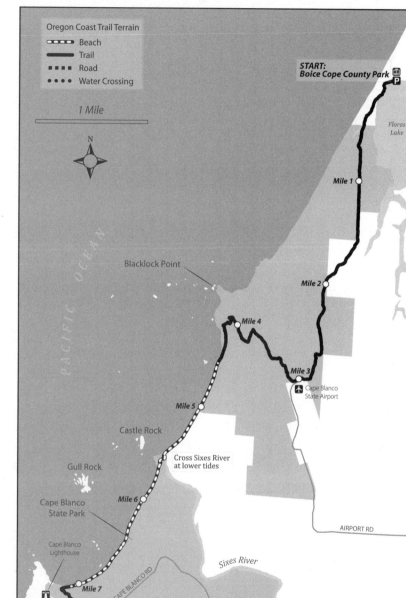

DAY 33

Cape Blanco State Park
to Paradise Point State Recreation Site

Distance: 5.6 miles

Terrain: Trail, beach

Begin: Cape Blanco State Park

Directions: From US Highway 101, turn west between mileposts 296 and 297 onto Cape Blanco Road and continue 5 miles until reaching the small parking area just before the gated road leading to the lighthouse.

End: Paradise Point State Recreation Site

Directions: From US Highway 101, turn west at the blinking light near milepost 300 onto Paradise Point Road and follow it until it veers to the right and ends at a small gravel parking area.

Overview

The day's hike begins where yesterday's left off, at Cape Blanco Lighthouse. For the more adventurous and ambitious, it is possible to combine Days 32 and 33 as a single hike, keeping in mind that two rivers need to be crossed at low or lower tides.

Description

Cross the road from the parking area and walk about 50 yards to the east to pick up the South Cape Trail. This lovely trail, high on a scenic bluff, continues as a grassy path for 0.3 mile and then turns inward, to the woods, and through a tunnel of dense vegetation. At 0.75 mile, turn right when you come to a paved road, and follow it 0.5 mile to Cape Blanco Beach.

If you happen to be camping in the park, another trail leads to the beach from the campground.

You will reach the Elk River after walking about 0.8 mile on the beach. Wade it at or near low tides, and continue walking on the beach 3.5 miles to Paradise Point State Recreation Site. The sand here is sloped and soft and difficult for walking.

• •

Cape Blanco Lighthouse was built in 1870 and is the oldest lighthouse still standing on the Oregon coast. The station was automated in 1980. Cape Blanco Lighthouse is owned by the US Coast Guard and is open for tours April through October, Wednesday through Monday (closed Tuesday).

• •

DAY 34

Paradise Point State Recreation Site to Humbug Mountain State Park

Distance: 9.6 miles

Terrain: Road, beach, highway, trail

Begin: Paradise Point State Recreation Site

Directions: From US Highway 101, turn west at the blinking light near milepost 300 onto Paradise Point Road and follow it until it veers to the right and ends at a small gravel parking area.

End: Humbug Mountain State Park

Directions: From US Highway 101, turn into Humbug Mountain State Park's day-use area between mileposts 307 and 308. The parking area is immediately adjacent to the highway.

Overview

Today's hike offers a couple of routing options, dependent in part on the tides and also on your willingness to negotiate a large field of rocks and boulders as a tradeoff for avoiding a stretch of walking along the highway. I also suggest a walking route through town in lieu of more beach walking. In any case, it is a diverse hike and offers a glimpse of the town of Port Orford as well as time on a lovely beach. The OCT continues on an old road and on trails weaving through Humbug Mountain State Park.

Description

Option 1—Town Walking: This guide suggests you explore the back streets of Port Orford for 2.25 miles rather than continuing on the beach from Paradise Point. Begin by following Paradise Point Road east out of the wayside until reaching Arizona Street. Turn right and walk on Arizona until it ends at an intersection with Pinehurst Drive. Turn left and then right onto Idaho Street. Walk along Idaho to 15th Street, and veer left for a brief digression to visit the short but interesting Port Orford Wetlands Interpretive Walkway. Resume walking on Idaho to 13th Street and turn left to reach US Highway 101. Walk south through town along the sidewalk to the Battle Rock Park (which is also referred to as Battle Rock Park Wayfinding Point).

A boat is hoisted on the dolly dock in Port Orford. (Photo by Lance Nix)

When walking through Port Orford, it's worth a short detour to turn right on Harbor Drive, which turns into Dock Road. Follow it to the end to see the dry ("dolly") dock.

Port Orford's dolly dock hoists boats into and out of the water each day. Only six such docks remain in the world, and two of these are on the West Coast (the other is in Los Angeles). Boats can't stay in the water overnight at Port Orford, because the harbor has no bar at its mouth to protect it from the elements.

Day 34: Paradise Point State Recreation Site to Humbug Mountain State Park

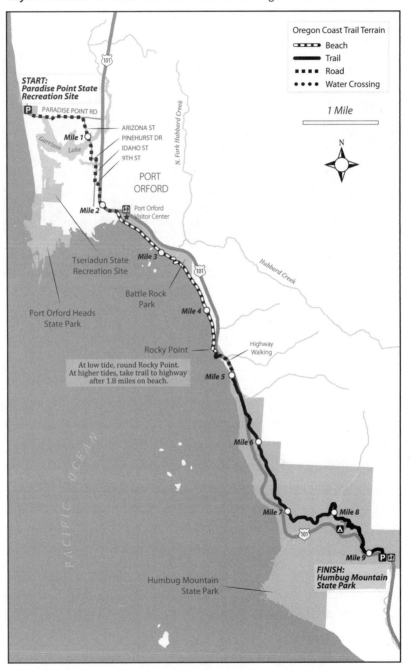

The rocks at Rocky Point are tricky to navigate. (Photo by Gordy Molitor)

Option 2—Beach Walking: Or, if you prefer, continue from Paradise Point south for 1 mile on the beach. This is difficult sand to walk on, but the beach is known for its agates, pretty rocks, and immediate views of Garrison Lake to the east. The beach ends at Tseriadun State Recreation Site. From there, follow Agate Beach Road, which becomes 9th Street, out of the park 0.75 miles to US Highway 101, and get back on the beach at Battle Rock Park.

After walking on the beach for 1.8 miles, you will come to a decision point, which puts you between a rock and a hard spot.

Option 1—higher tides: After 1.8 miles on the beach, a marked trail leads up to US Highway 101, and you can walk along the highway shoulder until accessing Humbug Mountain State Park on the other side of the highway after about 1.5 miles. This option is required at higher tides, and although walking along the shoulder of US Highway 101 is never pleasant, it may be preferable, even at low tide, to scrambling over rocks, as described below.

Option 2—low or lower tides: After 2.25 miles on the beach, if it is at or near low tide, you will come to Rocky Point, which can be rounded by scrambling over a large field of rocks—big rocks, small rocks, sharp

Trails on Humbug Mountain showcase indigenous varieties of ferns.

rocks, smooth rocks, but no soft rocks. At lower tides it's possible to get through the saddle of the point, only to find another field of rocks on the other side. Altogether, it is 0.75 miles of negotiating the rocks until they give way to sand. Although scrambling over the rocks is not especially difficult, it is cumbersome and slow, requiring good footing with every step. Even at low tide, some may prefer to exit the beach earlier (per Option 1, above) and walk along the highway rather than taking the time to cross the rock fields.

Once on the beach after crossing the rocks, walk a short distance (less than 0.25 mile), until reaching a path heading up the brushy hillside to a gravel road and small wayside just off US Highway 101. Follow the highway shoulder south 0.2 mile, and then cross the highway to a road with an OCT sign that takes off just past the entrance sign for Humbug Mountain State Park.

Follow the road (this is part of the old coast highway) for 2.6 miles as it curves around to the right, stay right at the split in the road, and walk through the gate. Do not take the path that leads to the campground. Instead, stay on the road and pass through another metal gate.

Immediately to the left, take the Day-Use Trail, which is marked with an OCT sign. It goes uphill, steeply at times, and drops down to parallel Brush Creek. Continue along this trail—a living laboratory for huge clumps of maidenhair, bracken, leather, sword, and coastal ferns—for 2 miles. Just as you think you're about to reach the highway, the trail climbs again but finally drops down to the creek and under the highway to a little path leading back to the day-use area.

DAY 35

Ophir Wayside State Park Rest Area to Rogue River North Jetty

Distance: 9.9 miles

Terrain: Beach, trail, road

Begin: Ophir Wayside State Park Rest Area

Directions: From US Highway 101, turn west at the blinking light at milepost 319. A small parking area is available.

End: Rogue River North Jetty

Directions: From US Highway 101, between mileposts 327 and 238, exit onto Wedderburn Loop just north of the Rogue River Bridge and follow signs to the Rogue River North Jetty. There is ample parking.

Curry Public Transit provides service between North Bend and Brookings; special stops along US Highway 101 may be arranged with advance notice and at the discretion of the driver.

This guide suggests eliminating 11 miles of US Highway 101 walking between Humbug Mountain and Ophir Wayside State Park Rest Area. This is the longest gap of the Oregon Coast Trail, and while it is possible to walk some portions of it on the beach, for the most part it would require walking along the shoulder of the highway.

Overview

This day begins and ends on sand, and in between offers a nice variety of old highway and trail walking as well as a visit to a historic gravesite. It is worth a very short detour to picnic or otherwise enjoy the panoramic views atop Otter Point.

Description

Begin the hike at the Ophir Wayside State Park Rest Area. From the parking area, take a short paved trail down to the beach and walk south 1.5 miles to the community of Nesika Beach. The sand is coarse and soft, making it somewhat more difficult to walk on during high tide when the beach is sloped. To exit the beach, look for a small saddle between two rock outcroppings and follow a little trail up to where Nesika Road begins. Turn right to follow that road south to where it meets US Highway 101 in another 1.5 miles. Do not take the first left turn because it will lead to the highway sooner than is needed.

Just before Nesika Road terminates at the highway, look for an OCT marker leading into a wooded trail on the right (south) side of the road. Take the path for 0.2 mile, where it ends at the Geisel Monument State Heritage Site, which is a memorial to the family of John Geisel, some of whom were killed in a Rogue Indian war skirmish. Picnic tables in this shaded and quiet spot provide a place to enjoy a brief respite. The road at the right-hand side of the family grave will take you to the highway. Turn right and walk just inside the guardrail until it ends, in about 0.2 mile. Then carefully cross the highway to access the Old Coast Road, which is clearly marked.

Follow this one-lane country road as it winds around houses, forest, and meadows until it reaches US Highway 101 again in 2 miles. Cross the highway and follow Otter Point Road 0.2 mile to Otter Point State Recreation Site. You will soon come to a fork in the road—the trail continues to the left, but it is well worth a slight detour to go straight ahead to enjoy a picnic or brief respite atop the bluff to better enjoy the panoramic and dramatic views. Retrace your steps back to the fork to continue on the main path, as there is no access to the beach from the bluff.

From the fork, take the pleasant wooded trail for about 0.5 mile to the beach. Follow the beach—a lovely composition of low dunes, bleached driftwood, and massive rock formations looming just off shore—for 3 miles south until it ends at the Rogue River north jetty. Scramble onto the jetty and walk on top of it the short distance to the parking area.

Day 35: Ophir Wayside State Park Rest Area to Rogue River North Jetty

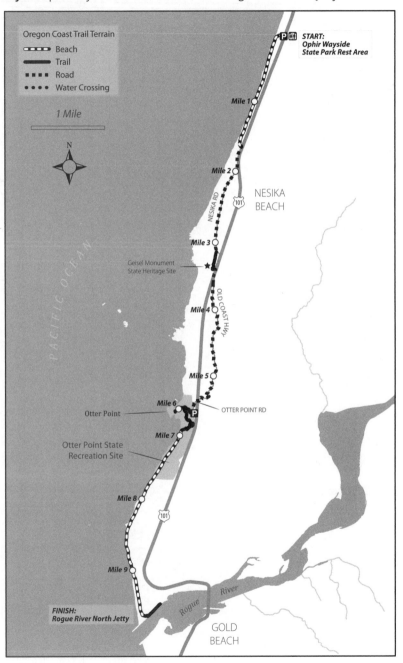

Oregon Coast Trail Terrain
- Beach
- Trail
- Road
- Water Crossing

1 Mile

N

START:
*Ophir Wayside
State Park Rest Area*

Mile 1

Mile 2

NESIKA RD

101

NESIKA
BEACH

PACIFIC OCEAN

Mile 3

Geisel Monument
State Heritage Site

OLD COAST HWY

Mile 4

Mile 5

Mile 6

Otter Point

P

OTTER POINT RD

Mile 7

Otter Point State
Recreation Site

Mile 8

101

Mile 9

Rogue River

FINISH:
Rogue River North Jetty

GOLD
BEACH

DAY 36

Rogue River North Jetty
to Cape Sebastian State Scenic Corridor

Distance: 11.4 miles

Terrain: Road, beach, trail

Begin: Rogue River North Jetty

Directions: From US Highway 101, exit onto Wedderburn Loop between mileposts 326 and 327, just north of the Rogue River Bridge, and follow signs to the Rogue River North Jetty. There is ample parking.

End: Cape Sebastian State Scenic Corridor

Directions: About 3 miles south of Gold Beach, take the exit for Cape Sebastian State Scenic Corridor off US Highway 101, between mileposts 333 and 334. Follow the signs to the south parking area.

Curry Public Transit provides service between North Bend and Brookings; special stops along US Highway 101 may be arranged with advance notice and at the discretion of the driver.

Overview

This wonderful day of hiking starts by crossing a McCullough bridge, and then you will stroll along the marina in Gold Beach to the beach for a nice stretch of walking. The hike ends with a strenuous but very scenic trail hike to the top of Cape Sebastian.

The total elevation gain for this hike is 1,561 feet, and the total elevation loss is 863 feet.

Description

Begin the hike by walking up Wedderburn Loop Road at the Rogue River

When crossing the bridge over the Rogue River, hikers should appreciate the ornate designs.

north jetty parking area to the Rogue River Bridge. Also known as the Isaac Lee Patterson Bridge, it was named for Oregon's governor from 1927 to 1929 and is one of a series of coastal bridges designed by Conde McCullough. Walk across the bridge—admiring the art deco motif—turn right at the first opportunity, onto Harbor Way, and walk through the marina area, where you'll find opportunities for food or restrooms. Turn right again at the post office onto S Jetty Road and follow it as it winds south past an RV park to where the beach starts at the south jetty. By now you will be about 2.8 miles into the hike.

Hike the beach, which can be difficult sand at high tide, past Hunter Creek, and continue walking. When you have gone a total of 7.5 miles (about 4.7 miles on the beach) and are nearing the end of the beach, start looking for a trail leading up to the top of Cape Sebastian State Scenic Corridor, which is indicated by a wooden post with the OCT logo set a distance off the beach on the hillside. From here it is about 4 miles to the top of Cape Sebastian.

Hike 1 mile on the trail, which is actually an old road that was once privately owned, to a signed junction; turn right and ignore the path that

Day 36: Rogue River North Jetty to Cape Sebastian State Scenic Corridor

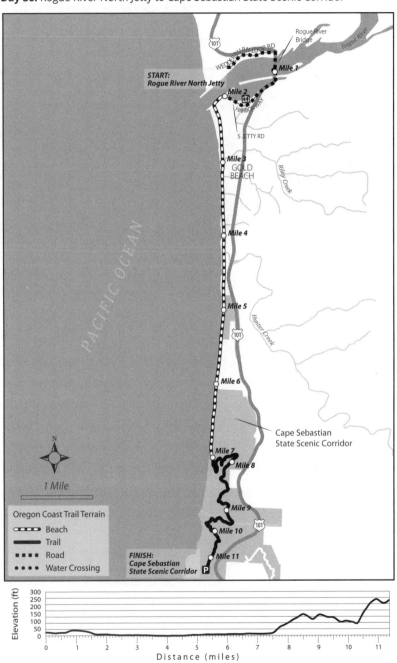

An Oregon park ranger admires the view atop Cape Sebastian.

leads left and up the hill. The trail descends and then ascends to another intersection. Go right again (down) until you emerge at a grassy viewpoint. Here, take a narrow and relentlessly steep trail up for 0.5 mile, with an occasional glimpse of the ocean. You will then enter a dark and atmospheric forest where the wind rattles through the trees. Meander along the wooded trail for about 0.5 mile farther, parallel to the road, and end at the Cape Sebastian south parking area.

DAY 37

Cape Sebastian State Scenic Corridor to Pistol River State Scenic Viewpoint

Distance: 5.6 miles

Terrain: Trail, beach

Begin: Cape Sebastian State Scenic Corridor

Directions: About 3 miles south of Gold Beach, take the exit for Cape Sebastian State Scenic Corridor off US Highway 101, between mileposts 333 and 334. Follow the signs to the south parking area.

End: Pistol River State Scenic Viewpoint

Directions: From US Highway 101, between mileposts 339 and 340, turn west into the wayside for Pistol River State Scenic Viewpoint.

Curry Public Transit provides service between North Bend and Brookings; special stops along US Highway 101 may be arranged with advance notice and at the discretion of the driver.

Overview

This hike takes you down the south side of Cape Sebastian and onto the beautiful, pristine Hunters Cove beach, ending with a wade across the Pistol River. Although not strictly tide dependent, it is better to avoid high tide for walking Hunters Cove beach in order to better wander through and among the seastacks. This hike has an elevation loss of 854 feet, all within the first 2 miles.

Description

Begin the hike by resuming the trail at the Cape Sebastian State Scenic Corridor south parking area and head south on a paved path at the OCT sign.

Hikers along Hunters Cove beach head south toward Pistol River.

The path transitions into a wooded trail in about 0.2 mile and immediately opens up to panoramic views to the north for you to experience the satisfaction of seeing what you accomplished on the previous hike. The trail descends through a lovely tunnel of trees, dense with salal, huckleberry, ferns, and other indigenous vegetation. It continues at a moderate grade for 1.7 miles; you'll then cross a little bridge and descend to the beach at Hunters Cove by use of a rope down the last bit of steep slope. Hunters Cove beach is remarkable for its rock formations just off or on the shore. Some can be walked around or through at lower tides.

Continue on the beach between the ocean and the Pistol River, which can't be seen over the low dunes, although the highway will be within eyesight and earshot. When you reach a large, pond-like body of water directly adjacent to a bridge on US Highway 101, which is actually part of the Pistol River, walk around the edge of the water and cross the dunes. When the parking area across the water is in sight, take off shoes and socks to wade across the shallow river. The parking area is straight ahead.

Day 37: Cape Sebastian State Scenic Corridor to Pistol River State Scenic Viewpoint

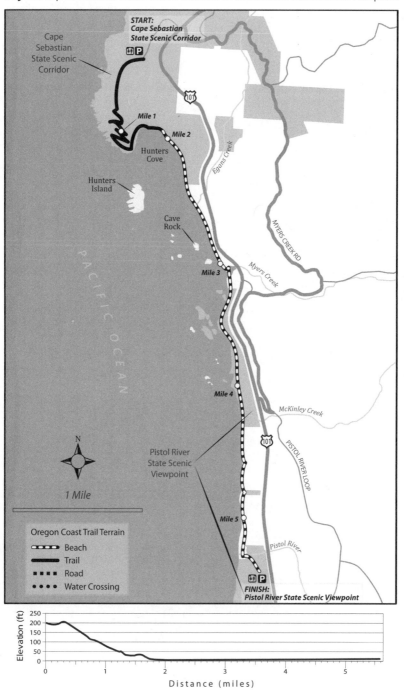

DAY 38

Arch Rock Picnic Area
to Whaleshead Beach Picnic Area

Distance: 8.6 miles

Terrain: Trail, beach

Begin: Arch Rock Picnic Area

Directions: Turn west into Arch Rock Picnic Area from US Highway 101 between mileposts 344 and 345.

End: Whaleshead Beach Picnic Area

Directions: Turn west into the Whaleshead Beach Picnic Area from US Highway 101 between mileposts 349 and 350.

Curry Public Transit provides service between North Bend and Brookings; special stops along US Highway 101 may be arranged with advance notice and at the discretion of the driver.

This guide recommends skipping 5.5 miles of what would be mostly highway walking from Pistol River State Scenic Viewpoint to Arch Rock Picnic Area. The OCT trail does extend about a mile north of Arch Rock, but can only be accessed from the south via the highway.

Overview

This is the first of two days through the Samuel H. Boardman State Scenic Corridor, and you will traverse through many beautiful and scenic waysides—Spruce Island, Secret Beach, Thunder Rock Cove, Natural Bridges, China Beach, Indian Sands, and Whaleshead Beach. The hiking is challenging, with many ups and downs, sometimes steep. Although this is a linear park, the trails are not. Numerous spur trails can be confusing, as they are not always clearly marked.

It is important to time reaching China Beach at low tide, or at least no later than mid-tide. After that, you will reach another highlight—walking across the Thomas Creek Bridge, the highest bridge in Oregon.

The total elevation gain for this hike is 1,853 feet, and the total elevation loss is 1,962 feet.

Description

Begin the hike by heading east from the parking area to the trailhead, which is situated just before you reach the highway. Proceed south on the trail, and in 0.4 mile you'll come to the Spruce Island parking lot, and then the trail rolls along a cliff edge with panoramic views of the coast. At 0.8 mile, when you reach a trail juncture, make a sharp left turn uphill. The trail heads back next to the highway, with moderate elevation gains and losses, then down to the juncture of a spur trail leading to Secret Beach, which you'll reach at about 1.5 miles into the hike. It is well worth dropping down onto this little pocket beach to explore it further, but there is no egress, so you will need to retrace your steps. The way down to and up from the beach requires negotiating some steep rocks, but is entirely doable.

If you do visit Secret Beach, return to the main trail and take a wooden footbridge across Miner Creek and up toward the Thunder Rock Cove parking area. South of the Thunder Rock Cove parking area, the trail continues toward the Natural Bridges parking area and then down to Natural Bridges. It then continues through a woodsy setting within earshot of US Highway 101 and with short segments along the highway shoulder, but these are all behind the guardrail.

The trail descends to China Beach at 3.9 miles into the hike, which you must reach by low or, at the latest, mid-tide, as the rocks cannot otherwise be rounded. The descent to China Beach is a little tricky and requires scrambling down some rocks to reach it. This is another remote and picturesque beach complete with a series of unique seastacks. Walk along the beach until reaching its egress about 0.25 mile from its southern end. Take the well-defined trail above a large pile of driftwood—it's the only option—and head up the steep hillside.

Day 38: Arch Rock to Whaleshead Beach

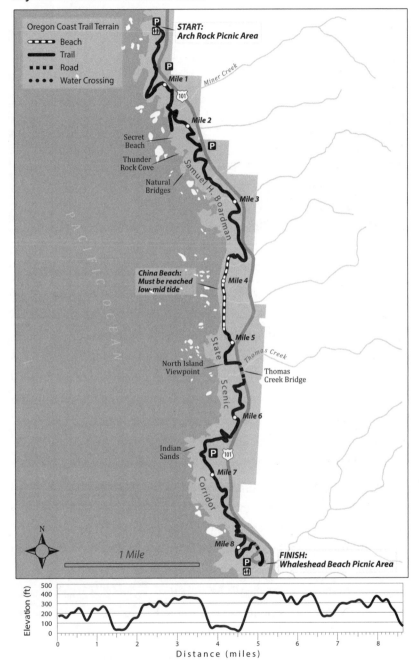

China Beach in Samuel H. Boardman State Scenic Corridor must be reached at lower tides.

From here, the first 0.5 mile or so is uphill, and then the terrain levels out. Continue toward the highway and the North Island viewpoint. Walk the highway shoulder a short distance to reach the Thomas Creek Bridge, the highest bridge in the state of Oregon. Walk single file along the narrow pedestrian pathway along the bridge. At the south end of the Thomas Creek Bridge parking area, locate the OCT markers and head south for views of hidden beaches and cliffs. Where there are junctions, keep to the south. The trail here is lush and dense, prolific with purple fungi, large banana slugs, and trees dripping with moss—primeval and wonderful.

At mile 6.75, you'll emerge from a tunnel of trees to enter a dramatically different landscape of open sands and sandstone cliffs. Indian Sands is an archaeological site that is listed on the National Register of Historic Places, and there is evidence of human activity dating back more than ten thousand years. Walk through the sand and, when you soon reach a trail juncture, continue straight ahead, where an old wooden OCT post will guide your way. (A left turn would take you to the Indian Sands parking area.)

The last part of the hike continues through woods and emerges onto the gravel road heading to Whaleshead Beach; cross the road to find the OCT, which drops down a grassy trail to the picnic and beach area, where the hike ends.

DAY 39

Whaleshead Beach Viewpoint
to Harris Beach State Park

Distance: 7.9 miles

Terrain: Trail, beach, highway, road

Begin: Whaleshead Beach Viewpoint

Directions: From US Highway 101, turn west between mileposts 349 and 350 into the Whaleshead Beach Viewpoint.

End: Harris Beach State Park

Directions: From US Highway 101, between mileposts 355 and 356, take the exit west into Harris Beach State Park. Park in the day-use parking lot, where there are also restrooms.

Curry Public Transit provides service between North Bend and Brookings; special stops along US Highway 101 may be arranged with advance notice and at the discretion of the driver.

Overview

The hike this day continues through the Boardman Corridor—though there are still ups and downs, it is more moderate than the previous hike. The scenic corridor ends at Rainbow Rock Condominiums, and it is highway and road walking from there for about 2 miles into Harris Beach State Park. This is also an area of the OCT that needs better signage; be especially attentive where there are spur trails.

While the previous hike ends at the Whaleshead Beach Picnic Area, this hike begins 0.25 mile farther south, at the Whaleshead Beach Viewpoint, because the trail from the Picnic Area is often closed due to erosion.

Description

Begin the hike by finding the OCT sign adjacent to the trail on the south side of the Whaleshead Beach Viewpoint parking area. For the first mile or so, the trail parallels the highway at a moderate grade, at times coming within a few yards of it and meandering along the shoulder for short spurts. At 1.3 miles, a spur trail heads south to the beach; don't take it. Instead, continue straight along the woodsy pathway with its ups and downs, and cross a couple of wooden bridges before reaching House Rock Viewpoint just past 2 miles. At the south end of the rock wall, look for an OCT sign and take the trail that heads west toward the ocean then north a short distance before making an S turn and veering south. (Do not take a trail that heads south and down into the woods.)

The OCT continues south about 1.5 miles toward Cape Ferrelo through a mix of open fields and woods. At Cape Ferrelo, find the route on the south side of the wayside, and at the fork in the trail, which comes soon, turn right to find an OCT sign. Continue to the Lone Ranch Picnic Area and drop down to the beach. Walk the length of the beach about 0.5 mile, and just past the large rock outcropping in the ocean, the trail heads fairly steeply up the headland. Climb up and along the spine of the headland; it then enters a dense forest. Follow it through the woods about a mile until it emerges just behind a condominium complex, where the lovely Samuel H. Boardman State Scenic Corridor ends and the OCT rudely deposits hikers at the edge of the busy US Highway 101.

Walk 1 mile on the west shoulder of the highway until you reach Dawson Road. A multiuse bicycle and pedestrian path links the highway directly to Harris Beach State Park, emerging after about a mile at the entrance to the campground. Continue to the day-use area parking, where the hike ends.

Day 39: Whaleshead Beach Viewpoint to Harris Beach State Park

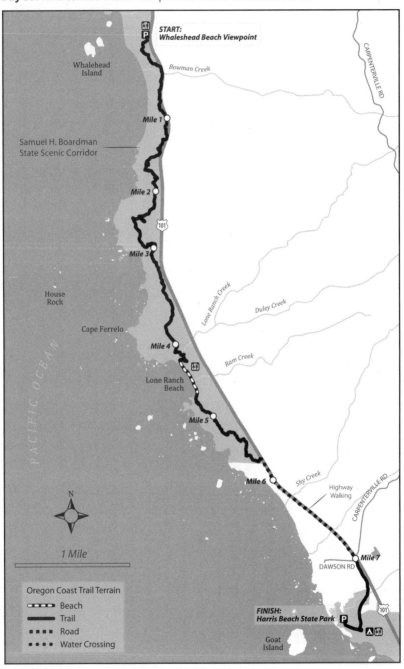

Samuel Boardman

Establishing the Oregon Parks System

IN 1913, THE SAME YEAR THE OREGON BEACHES WERE DECLARED A HIGH-way, the Oregon State Highway Commission was established to oversee the construction of state roads. Work on the coastal highway—named the Roosevelt Coast Military Highway in honor of President Theodore Roosevelt, who died in 1919—began in 1921 and was funded in part by a state gasoline tax enacted in 1919, the country's first. It was later renamed the Oregon Coast Highway; officially it is now US Highway 101. With the advent of the auto and more reliable roads, more people enjoyed the beaches for recreation and tourism flourished in coastal communities.

The legislature subsequently authorized the Highway Commission to acquire rights-of-way along state highways for "the maintenance and preservation of scenic beauty." To begin with, several small parks and waysides were purchased. These efforts were expanded, and the highway commissioners became directors of a parks system and managers of the beaches, an arrangement that lasted until 1990, when a separate parks department was established.

At an age when many people begin to contemplate retirement, Samuel Boardman began a productive and fruitful career that spanned twenty-one years. In 1929, when he was fifty-five years old, Boardman assumed the position as first superintendent of Oregon State Parks, and ever since Oregonians have benefited from his vision, dedication, and foresight. Prior to this appointment, he worked for the state in road construction and led efforts for a major tree-planting campaign in Eastern Oregon. The town

Samuel Boardman, first superintendent of Oregon State Parks, relaxes in suit and tie at Spring Creek, 1945. (Photo courtesy OPRD)

of Boardman, located in Morrow County, and where he homesteaded, is named for him.

Acquiring Coastal Property

In hiking the Oregon Coast Trail, walkers traverse multiple state parks and scenic waysides or recreation areas that are owned and overseen by the State of Oregon. The proximity of these parks and waysides makes it possible to get to the shore all along the coast (an advantage that is sorely lacking in most other coastal states) or to enjoy it from scenic sites easily accessible by car.

Boardman acquired many of these parks, including Short Sand Beach (renamed Oswald West State Park in 1958), Ecola, Cape Lookout, Sunset Bay, Shore Acres, Cape Arago, Humbug Mountain, and of course the Samuel H. Boardman State Scenic Corridor.

In 1927, before Boardman's appointment, Oregon had 4,070 acres in forty-six small state parks. During his tenure, Boardman concentrated on acquiring new park lands throughout the state, especially along the coast. At his retirement, there were 181 parks, and acreage had increased to 66,000. Lands were obtained through a variety of methods. Cape Lookout was a gift from the US Lighthouse Service; lands composing Ecola State Park were obtained through gifts, purchase, and third-party negotiations; Cape Arago was given to the state in 1932 by Louis and Lela Simpson, Coos

County, and the Cape Arago Park Commission; and Sunset Bay State Park was acquired because of unpaid taxes (Boardman had happened to see an advertisement in the newspaper for its sale).

Sometimes individual parcels were obtained and over time combined and developed into parks. Land for what is now Oswald West State Park, for example, was first acquired through a donation by lumberman and philanthropist E. S. Collins. Back taxes were paid on property located on Neahkahnie Mountain, and the state purchased portions of additional pieces of property at a low price. Boardman must have been persuasive, as well as patient, to convince landowners to part with their property in the best interest of the state. He also had to convince his own bosses to appropriate money for land acquisition at a time when pressure to put all the funds in highway construction was great. In recollecting his efforts to create Short Sand Beach State Park (now Oswald West State Park), Boardman wrote:

On September 19, 1949, I brought it again before the Commission. This time they voted to purchase the property at $50 an acre, with stern orders that I was not to bring any further acquisitions relating to Short Sand Beach Park before them. An eight-year love's labor won for one unit of a park. What could have been wrong with me!

And about the same park, he also wrote:

Short Sand Beach Park contains today 2,401 acres costing $91,000. Today's recreational value can only be computed by an extended slide rule. One hundred years from today and all the gold buried in the Knox caves would be but pennies. Such things cannot be judged in currency. What is the value of a soul?

In the early 1940s, Boardman proposed that an extensive area along the Curry County coastline be designated as a national park, an idea that did not reach fruition because of the lack of federal funds and because local cattle owners did not want to lose grazing ground. A state park—a twelve-mile linear scenic corridor—was developed, however, which today includes the coastal frontage proposed for the national park and was named for Boardman at the time of his retirement. The Samuel H. Boardman State Scenic Corridor is traversed on days 38 and 39, and these are among the most spectacular hikes of the entire journey.

Boardman was concerned primarily with acquiring new park lands, and he placed more emphasis on land protection than its management. He did not encourage the development of facilities such as picnic areas or camping sites, preferring instead to preserve the land in its natural state. As he wrote, "I have gathered unto the state, creations of the great Architect. Guardedly, I have kept these creations as they were designed. When man enters the field of naturalness, the artificial enters." He was succeeded as parks superintendent by Chester Armstrong in 1950, who was charged with expanding park development for public use.

Sam Boardman traveled about 500,000 miles while building and managing the parks system. We know this because he kept meticulous records of his travels, meetings, and activities related to park oversight. He retired as state parks superintendent in 1950 at age seventy-six. After that, he spent part of each day in the Parks Division office writing historic anecdotes and amusing descriptions of some of the parks as well as documenting how they were acquired. Some of these stories were published in 1954 by the Oregon Historical Society in a small booklet: *Oregon State Park System: A Brief History*.

DAY 40

Harris Beach State Park
to Crissey Field State Recreation Site

Distance: 8.9 miles

Terrain: Trail, road, beach

Begin: Harris Beach State Park

Directions: From US Highway 101, between mileposts 355 and 356, take the exit west into Harris Beach State Park. Park in the day-use parking lot, where there are also restrooms.

End: Just beyond Crissey Field State Recreation Site (California Border)

Directions: On US Highway 101, turn right at milepost 362. Continue on the road until reaching the Welcome Center's large parking area.

Curry Public Transit provides bus service between Brookings and Smith River, California, along US Highway 101. It may be possible to prearrange for a drop-off or pickup at the entrance to Crissey Field State Recreation Site and/or within Brookings.

Overview

California is in sight! The final day is fairly easy and combines an urban walk through town and along back roads. Fittingly, you will enter California on the beach, though there is no official "line in the sand." The routing for the end of this hike is tide dependent. At low tide, it is possible to enter the beach at McVay Rock State Recreation Site and continue all the way on the beach. At higher tides, some highway walking is required.

Description

Begin the hike by walking from the day-use parking area of Harris Beach

State Park to the south end of the park to find a paved walking path. Follow it until it transitions to sidewalk adjacent to the highway, and walk 2.1 miles into Brookings, crossing the Chetco River Bridge. Take the first right turn off the bridge to Lower Harbor Road and continue 1 mile through the harbor area. Stay on Lower Harbor Road, take it uphill to the left, walk to Oceanview Drive, and turn right. This road parallels Highway 101 for 3.5 miles and travels through scenic farmlands to the entrance of McVay Rock State Recreation Site. From here, it's only 2 miles to California.

Option 1—low or lower tides: At lower tides it is possible to enter the beach at McVay Rock State Recreation Site and continue all the way to California on the beach. A trail leads down from the bluff for 0.2 mile to the pebbly beach. A small rocky point about 0.5 mile south on the beach can be passed only at low tide, so plan accordingly or be prepared for more road walking. After about 1 mile of rock scrambling, the rocks give way to sand. Continue along the beach and wade the Winchuck River. The last 0.5 mile to Crissey Field State Recreation Site is all on beach. Look for the contemporary building (this is the Welcome Center) set off the beach. The border is just past this site.

Option 2—high tide: At higher tides you won't be able to round the rocks at McVay Beach, and crossing the Winchuck River will also be more difficult, so continue walking along Oceanview Drive about another mile until it hits US Highway 101. Walk the shoulder south for 0.4 mile to just north of the Winchuck River. Head west along the access road to the beach, wade the river, and continue south on the beach.

The last 0.5 mile to Crissey Field State Recreation Site is all on beach. The border is just past the Welcome Center.

Although you won't know exactly where or exactly when, at some point in this hike, one foot will be in Oregon with the other poised to land in California. If this ends a journey that began at the mouth of the Columbia River, then savor the moment. Not many people can say they have walked the length of a state at the edge of a continent. Take off the backpack, unlace the hiking boots, and telescope the hiking poles back into place. Savor the moment.

Day 40: Harris Beach State Park to Crissey Field State Recreation Site

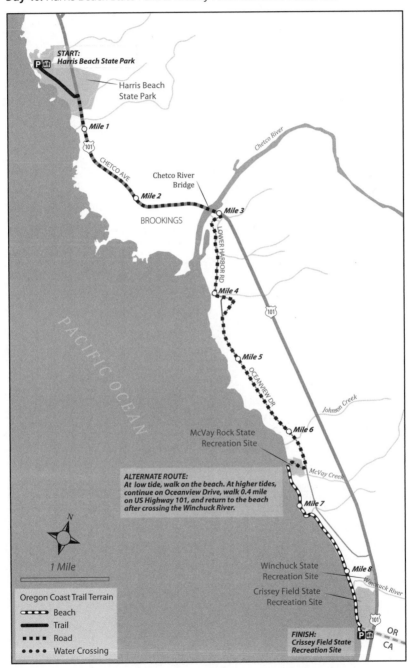

START:
Harris Beach State Park

Harris Beach
State Park

Mile 1

CHETCO AVE

Chetco River

Chetco River
Bridge

Mile 2

BROOKINGS

Mile 3

LOWER HARBOR RD

Mile 4

101

PACIFIC OCEAN

Mile 5

OCEANVIEW DR

Johnson Creek

Mile 6

McVay Rock State
Recreation Site

McVay Creek

ALTERNATE ROUTE:
*At low tide, walk on the beach. At higher tides,
continue on Oceanview Drive, walk 0.4 mile
on US Highway 101, and return to the beach
after crossing the Winchuck River.*

N

Mile 7

1 Mile

Winchuck State
Recreation Site

Mile 8

Winchuck River

Crissey Field State
Recreation Site

Oregon Coast Trail Terrain
Beach
Trail
Road
Water Crossing

FINISH:
*Crissey Field State
Recreation Site*

OR
CA

Trail Gaps and Opportunities

Trail Gaps

IT MAY SEEM INCONGRUOUS, EVEN WHILE PROMOTING THE VIRTUES OF THE
Oregon Coast Trail, to also point out its deficiencies. For, as wonderful
as it is to walk the entire OCT—and I cannot overstate how wonderful it
is—here's the thing: it could be better. Even after forty years, the OCT is
a work in progress. Someday it might be possible to walk the full length
of the coastal trail without having to negotiate the gaps that presently ex-
ist—gaps that force hikers either to interrupt their trek or to walk long
distances along a highway not designed for pedestrian use. Until then,
hikers should be cognizant of and prepare for those areas lacking a trail.

Some of the forty hikes presented in this book deviate from the official
Oregon Coast Trail in order to deliberately avoid what the OPRD considers
a "gap" in the trail. The approximately forty-five miles of identified gaps
are for the most part caused by rocky headlands, rivers or other bodies of
water, and the presence of private property where a trail would be needed.

Efforts are underway to mitigate these gaps by seeking grant funds to
build new trails or to negotiate agreements with other public or private
landowners. OPRD has identified both a short- and long-term solution
to address each gap, but the implementation process can be cumbersome,
costly, and time-consuming. Often, the short-term solution is to simply
improve the ability to walk along the highway. This may involve, for example, developing or expanding a bicycle lane, restriping and widening
the shoulder lane, installing pedestrian safety warning signs or signals, or
clearing vegetation to create a narrow pathway inside the guardrail.

Long-term solutions are the preferred solutions, but by definition are more complex and costly, and therefore more difficult to implement. They may entail building new trail on land owned by a public agency other than OPRD, such as the Oregon Department of Transportation or the US Forest Service, obtaining easements across private land, or formalizing boat shuttles as an official part of the OCT. For the most part, geographical constraints are not insurmountable, and viable solutions for overcoming them can usually be found. However, these solutions are patched together depending on how funding opportunities present themselves, which is not necessarily in a holistic manner.

Information Gaps

Making improvements to the OCT will be of little use if people don't know about them. Unfortunately there is often lag time from when the trail is changed to when directional markers are installed, or when written or online information is revised to reflect the changes.

Although the OCT is not a wilderness-based hike and walkers are not likely to go far off route, it is not always intuitive to know how to follow the trail, which can prove frustrating and a waste of time when left to wonder which way to turn or where exactly to get off the beach. A more comprehensive and coordinated approach for improving trail signage would greatly improve hikers' experiences by promoting a more seamless system of wayfinding.

While this sounds logical and good, a number of challenges prevent what would otherwise appear to be a straightforward improvement. The OCT incorporates many existing local trails (i.e., Tillamook Head, Amanda's Trail, the Hobbit Trail, etc.) with their own identity and names. Therefore, the OCT hiker needs to know, in and near Yachats, for example, to walk the 804 Trail to Amanda's Trail, connect to the St. Perpetua Trail, and then to the Captain Cook Trail to the Oregon Coast Trail until reaching Cummins Creek Road. In fact, *all* of these segments compose the OCT but are not always designated as such on maps or identified with consistent signage.

The requirement for an archaeological assessment to ensure the protection of ancient artifacts may also delay any trail construction or improvement, including the placement of signs. Efforts have been made to minimize impact by using lighter and thinner poles, but their placement is still an issue. It's difficult or impossible to place markers in the sand for hikers to know where to get off the beach. Sometimes markers are placed just off the beach on more solid ground, but they can be hard to spot from the beach. Sometimes markers get pried off the posts and stolen. Sometimes local residents object to the markers placed near their homes or businesses. Sometimes local park personnel assigned to trail maintenance and sign placement have other priorities and may not get around to it in a timely manner.

OPRD has not adopted but should consider approaches utilized by other long-distance trails, such as placing markers or blazes on trees or rocks. In fact, any combination of techniques, so long as signage is consistent and uniquely identified with the OCT, should be incorporated into OPRD protocols.

Untapped Opportunities

When the Oregon Coast Trail was first envisioned in the early 1970s, it was considered a high priority for completion because of its perceived potential to enhance economic development along the coast. Indeed, a great appeal in hiking the OCT is in visiting Oregon's coastal communities that are off the beaten path. The hikes in this guide encourage exploring neighborhoods or back roads along the route in order to better appreciate each town's unique characteristics. Hikers are directed through portions of many towns where there are opportunities to enjoy a meal, visit gift shops, or arrange for lodging. This type of low-impact ecotourism can financially benefit local communities; in fact, most of them already rely heavily on the tourist industry.

It's impossible to fully realize the OCT's potential to enhance economic development because there is not an accurate count of how many people use the trail each year or, of those who do hike some or all of it, what new revenues are generated as a result of their visits. OPRD staff estimates, based on anecdotal evidence, that approximately one thousand people per year complete at least some through-hiking (more than a day) on the trail. This equates to fewer than three people per day or, even if realistically assuming that most visits occur during the one hundred days of best weather, ten people per day. (Of course, many more people complete day hikes that are part of the OCT. In particular, trails over Tillamook Head, Cape Falcon, Neahkahnie Mountain, and Cape Lookout draw thousands of users each year.)

It would behoove OPRD to research and document basic assumptions about the OCT's usage and resulting economic impact in order to establish a baseline and measure its continued impact over time. Other trails and management systems can be a model for this. For example, Missouri State Parks, which manages the Katy Trail State Park—the nation's longest rail-trail project at 237 miles of bicycle and pedestrian trail—conducted a study to quantify the trail's benefits. It found that hundreds of businesses along the Katy Trail provide a variety of tourism-related services, from wineries, restaurants, and shops to bed and breakfasts inns, hotels, and campgrounds. And the economic impact they found was astoundingly positive: for every dollar spent by Missouri State Parks to operate Katy Trail State Park, Missouri's economy saw an $18 return on investment.

It's worth asking, then, what it would take to increase the number of through-hikers for the OCT, a goal that seems very attainable. These additional people are certain to support local economies in the form of purchasing food, equipment, or lodging.

Surely potential OCT hikers are discouraged by having to walk along a major highway not designed for pedestrian use. The hard work has been done. Some one hundred years ago, our beaches were saved from private ownership and dedicated for use by the public—beaches that form the spine of this journey. Fulfilling the promise of a seamless coastal trail will require an investment of time, technical skills, political will, and financial resources—but it can be done and will be worth the investment many times over. We deserve for a walk as wonderful as the Oregon Coast Trail to be both scenic and safe. Only then will it realize its full potential as a great distance hike, one that people will seek out and long remember.

Other States, Other Beaches

How unique are Oregon's policies regarding beach access? In a word: very. Only two other states—Texas and Hawaii—allow full public access to both the dry and wet sand portions of their beaches. And even in those states, legal, political, and ecological challenges threaten to erode the public's access.

Twenty-three of the country's fifty states (46 percent) border the Pacific Ocean, the Atlantic Ocean, or the Gulf of Mexico. Their shoreline areas range from 6,640 miles along Alaska's coastline to seventeen miles along New Hampshire's eastern boundary. It is estimated that half the population of the United States lives within fifty miles of the coast, but 70 percent of coastal land is privately owned, and the simple pleasure of walking on the beach is limited to those who can afford it.

In order to fully appreciate our open beaches (and it is perhaps too easy for Oregonians to take this privilege for granted), we need only examine a few other states' policies regarding beach access.

Texas

Texas is of interest because Oregon's Beach Bill was modeled after similar legislation, the Texas Open Beaches Act, enacted in 1959. Texas beaches span 367 miles along the Gulf of Mexico (similar in area to Oregon's coastline); there are approximately 360 public coastal access sites, or about one public access site for every mile of shoreline. Beach oversight is assigned to the General Land Office (GLO); its commissioner is elected statewide.

Texas beaches, such as this one in Port Bolivar, are open beaches.

In recent years some legislative and legal actions specific to the Open Beaches Act have challenged the limits of public rights to use the beaches in Texas. In 2005, Hurricane Rita hit the Gulf of Mexico, causing significant damage and erosion to beaches in Galveston, resulting in some houses ending up on wet sands—the public beach. One such homeowner was asked, and offered financial compensation, by the GLO to relocate her house off the public beach. She not only refused but also sued the state, claiming her rights as a private property owner were violated. The Texas Supreme Court, in a decision handed down in 2012, ruled in her favor. The ruling caused confusion about the definition of a public beach and consternation among those who feared their rights, as well as beaches, could be eroded one tropical storm at a time.

Hawaii

Only Alaska, Florida, and California have more shoreline than Hawaii. Although all beaches in Hawaii are owned by and open to the public, access is restricted in some locations by the development of hotels, condominiums, and private homes on beachfront properties. On all islands, access has been guaranteed by traditional public easements, but these are under constant restrictions or threat of loss. Private gates and security guards have been placed at some locations, and some private homes and developments have been encroaching on the public's right of way to the beaches by extending their vegetation line (sometimes by planting invasive and nonindigenous species) farther toward the ocean. This activity was declared illegal by a Hawaii Supreme Court ruling in 2006. The court further declared that the shoreline should be established "at the highest reach of the highest wash of the waves."

Maine

The coastal states of Delaware, Maine, Massachusetts, New Hampshire, and Virginia use the mean low tide line rather than the high tide line to demark the boundary between private and public property. These states do not own the intertidal zone of their beaches, and therefore private property owners can own land all the way down to the mean low tide line.

Maine is famous for its beautiful rocky shoreline populated with quaint villages and is home to Acadia National Park, which serves to showcase the state's shores. The vast majority (estimated at 95 percent) of Maine's 228 miles of shoreline is privately owned; in fact, there are only 27 miles of publically owned sandy beaches.

The public rights to beach access are subject to a centuries-old law, the Massachusetts Colonial Ordinance of 1641–47, applicable only to Maine and Massachusetts, which were originally one colony. This ordinance allows the public to use the intertidal zone for the limited purposes of "fishing, fowling, and navigation." Everything else—walking, picnicking, surfing, sunbathing, or just enjoying the view, for example—requires the permission of waterfront property owners, who can otherwise prosecute violators for trespassing.

The question as to what constitutes "fishing, fowling, and navigation" has been addressed on a case-by-case basis over the years. Fishing includes digging for worms and clams, and a person may be on privately owned tidal areas if engaged in these activities. The right to fish does not include the right to fasten fishing equipment on private property. Seaweed that is floating or growing in the sea can be harvested by the public, but once it accumulates on the beach, it belongs to the property owner. While fowling

Private property in Maine extends to the low water mark.

is generally interpreted to mean bird hunting, some have suggested that this definition should also include bird watching, but there has been no court ruling on this. With respect to navigation, the public can sail over intertidal lands, and vessels can rest upon the intertidal land when the tide is out. A person can walk on intertidal lands for purposes related to navigation or can swim in intertidal lands so long as the ground is not touched. Maine legal courts recently ruled in favor of a scuba diver to cross a section of intertidal flats owned by his neighbor to engage in scuba diving.

Massachusetts has similar restrictions to public use of its beaches.

New Jersey

The historic Jersey Shore encompasses 130 miles of coastline along the Atlantic Ocean. Most beaches in New Jersey are owned by local jurisdictions, referred to as boroughs or townships. These shore municipalities act as trustees of the state's beaches, managing them for the benefit of the public, and they are authorized to charge "reasonable fees" for beach access in order to fund services and facilities related to beach maintenance, safety, and recreation. Almost all boroughs and townships require the purchase of a beach tag to walk on or use the beach. Those walking on the beach without one can be fined for trespassing.

Some beach towns restrict access further by limiting parking and availability of public restrooms, designating specific areas of the beach for games and recreation, or establishing other rules, such as whether food can be taken onto the beach.

California

The battle for California's shoreline is primarily focused on public access to the beaches, a struggle that often pits the interests of the wealthy against those of the general public. As reported by the *San Francisco Chronicle* in October 2013, "A San Mateo County judge allowed a billionaire oceanfront property owner to block the only public access to a beach in Half Moon Bay that has been enjoyed for at least a century by fishermen, tourists, sunbathers, families and surfers. Although the public is still allowed to use the beach, the only way people can get there is from the ocean."

The enactment of the California Coastal Act of 1976 by the California legislature established guidelines to improve public access to the state's beaches. Prior to that, 600 of the 1,100 miles of coastline had been blocked off, denying access to virtually anyone other than those owning beachfront property. But progress has been slow and difficult. Many who are wealthy enough to own real estate along the California coast have used their financial resources to delay—through litigation or other tactics—implementation of rules that are intended to provide additional public easements to the beach.

The State of California owns the tide and land seaward of the "mean high tide," a definition that is virtually impossible to delineate. No one knows exactly where that is. In general, it is assumed that the public can use the wet sand areas of all the beaches, but it's often difficult to get to them. The California Coastal Act requires property owners to allow for public easements in exchange for permits for development.

Even when easements are in place, it's difficult for the public to know where they are because there may not be any signs to indicate where the public is allowed, and an easement in front of one house may be sandwiched between two houses without them. This is especially the case in the community of Malibu, which boasts a twenty-mile stretch of scenic beaches and where the community has been particularly recalcitrant in implementing the Coastal Act. In fact, the public is routinely discouraged from using the beaches by the placement of inaccurate "Private Beach" signs posted on houses, illegal placement of orange traffic cones to block parking, or the installation of gates or other barriers. In one case, a land-owner installed fake garage doors behind an illegal curb cut to discourage parking and public access.

While more easements have been opened since the passage of the California Coastal Act, a user's manual and navigational skills are some-times needed to determine where it is possible to walk on the beach. This is what prompted Jenny Price, an environmental writer and beach advocate, to develop a smart phone application, Our Malibu Beaches. This tool pro-vides basic information about the public's right to use the beaches, maps to often-hidden entry gates, and house-by-house descriptions showing public property boundaries. For example:

> 2nd house from accessway—can use dry sand for 25 ft from high tide line up to 10 feet from house. Ignore any wayward signs to the contrary.

> 4th house—big deck upcoast—can use dry sand in front of the house but not in front of the deck upcoast of the house for 25 feet from High Tide Line up to 5 ft from house

Florida

Florida's 1,100 miles of sandy beaches generate billions of dollars in tourism revenue annually. Over 60 percent of Florida's population lives within five miles of a beach, but there is only about one public access site for about every five miles of shoreline. This corresponds to roughly one access for every 10,000 residents. Sixty-seven percent of the beaches in Florida are privately owned.

Washington

Understanding public beach ownership and access laws in Washington State is a complicated endeavor and it can be confusing for the public to know where they are allowed to walk on the beach or where doing so is considered trespassing.

As with other states, regulations governing public and private ownership on Washington's shores date back to when it was granted statehood, in 1889. That same year, the state legislature elected to sell its tidelands and beaches, in large part to promote and encourage the shellfish industry. This practice continued until 1971, when state legislation was enacted to cease the sale of tidelands. Today, an estimated 60 to 70 percent of Washington's tidelands are in private hands, and public access is available to only about 30 percent of the state's shorelines, including the Puget Sound, the San Juan and other islands, and other beaches along the Pacific Ocean. With some exceptions, the beaches along the ocean shore are open to the public, with access primarily being a concern along the state's extensive inland waters.

Property owners may be private individuals, corporations, or nonprofit organizations; state, federal, or local governments; or Indian tribes. Each of these entities manages its beaches differently. Olympic National Park encompasses seventy-three miles along the ocean and is managed by the US National Park Service. Some state parks are located along the coast and are overseen by Washington State Parks, which also regulates recreational use of the shores they manage. Five separate tribes own beach property and control access to those beaches. The Quinault Indian Nation includes twenty-three miles of beach lands, but due to concerns about unauthorized use of the beaches, the tribe closed public access to them in 2012. Other tribes, such as the Makah, allow public access to the beaches with the purchase of a recreation permit. Some beaches are limited to use by tribal members because they are considered sacred or ceremonial sites.

Despite the fact that the state sold off the tidelands several decades after treaties were signed with Indian tribes in the 1850s, the treaty right to harvest shellfish remained intact. To this day, fifteen Indian tribes are entitled to half the shellfish harvest, even if that harvest occurs on private property.

Policing and Protecting the Shores

So it is that, unlike most other coastal states, all of Oregon's beaches—both the wet and the dry sands—are considered public beaches with no fee to use them and with few barriers preventing access to enjoy them. And enjoy them we do. It is estimated that 80 percent of Oregonians (pity the other 20 percent) visit the coast at least once a year—for inspiration, recreation, relaxation, or celebration. Ours is an inheritance worth the world's riches, and is a gift that can't be bought or sold.

Oregon's beaches are unique in another respect as well. The 1967 Beach Bill delegated the Oregon Parks and Recreation Department (originally the Oregon State Highway Commission) with the responsibility to "police, protect and maintain property that is subject to… this Act." No other state has designated a park agency to oversee its ocean shores. Most have assigned coastal oversight to a department of natural resources or one focused on environmental protection. But Oregon's beaches were considered roads, a fact explaining the direct relationship between the development of the coastal highway and the establishment of parks and public waysides. Even after 1965, when the shoreline was no longer considered a highway but rather a recreation area, it was still managed by the Highway Commission. It was not until 1990 that a separate parks department was formed.

The agency that oversees Oregon's parks today has greatly evolved from the days of Samuel Boardman. In 1940, just over 2 million people visited Oregon's parks, and 73 percent of these visits were to coastal parks. In 2013, over 43 million people visited Oregon parks, and half of these visits were to parks or waysides with beach access. With an annual budget of nearly $125 million, OPRD supports park operations with 857 employees (about half of these are seasonal or part-time workers). About one-third of the revenues to support the parks is generated from the state lottery, and other sources of funds include state registration of recreational vehicles and park user fees.

"Policing, protecting and maintaining" the shore entails a wide range of responsibilities, tasks, and activities, and the public may be unaware of some of them. These include, among other things:

- ensuring the beaches are free of debris and litter, including what is washed ashore by catastrophic events such as tsunamis;
- oversight of recreational use on the beaches, which can be complicated because regulations are not necessarily consistent among communities (a person may operate a bicycle, skateboard, scooter, rollerblades, or inline skates on the beach at Seaside, but may not play golf);
- disposing of dead sea mammals—about five whales wash ashore on Oregon beaches each year, not always in locations where it is convenient to bury them; and
- issuing permits for a variety of reasons, including for shore armoring, or riprap.

Oregon's beach rangers clean up debris and otherwise keep an eye on the beaches. (Photo courtesy of OPRD)

Four OPRD beach rangers are assigned to patrol Oregon's beaches— each ranger covers a territory of about one hundred miles in a truck,

Jeep, or ATV. Rangers focus their efforts in two main areas: beach safety for visitors through education of riptides, unstable cliffs, and other hazards; and protection of natural resources, which may entail plant restoration, closing illegal trails, and managing invasive plants.

Unlike park rangers in many other states (including Washington), Oregon's rangers are not considered law enforcement personnel and therefore do not carry firearms. Instead, they explain and enforce park regulations through education while relying on local law enforcement agencies to pursue violations if necessary. While it may prove challenging to patrol a large area of beach terrain—some beaches are difficult to access due to storms, tides, or other barriers—the "office" environment can't be beat.

Like other public agencies, OPRD must balance the interests of a wide range of constituents—interests that at times conflict with each other. Some who visit Oregon's beaches would prefer for them to remain as pristine and unspoiled as possible by, for example, establishing stricter zoning requirements to limit growth and promoting wildlife and environmental restoration. Another perspective, however, would favor economic development by building new roads or otherwise expanding infrastructure in coastal communities to attract new businesses. Some would favor completely prohibiting motorized vehicles on the beaches while others would support allowing a full range of recreational activities on the shores. Some would ban the presence of riprap in order to allow for the natural distribution of sand even if this results in the eventual destruction of houses; others see installation of riprap necessary in order to protect their property.

No one could deny these are difficult choices. Although Oregon's political history, especially when compared to eastern states, is not a lengthy one, its heritage is rich, steeped in tradition, and based on a deep appreciation of the state's beauty, unique and diverse landscapes, and its natural resources. These are the values that connect us to the land and define our sense of place. These, too, are values that must be regularly reaffirmed in order to best protect these precious resources both in the short term and for future generations.

Acknowledgments

THE FIRST PERSON I CONTACTED TO INITIATE THIS PROJECT WAS ROCKY
Houston, the state trails coordinator for the Oregon Parks and Recreation
Department. Rocky patiently answered my many questions, met with me
on numerous occasions, and made agency files about the Oregon Coast
Trail available to me. He never once indicated that he was too busy to
respond to my emails, that I was asking a stupid question, or that I was
in over my head—although I am sure all of these things were true at one
time or another.

The second person I contacted was Jack Remington, the first statewide
trails coordinator (Rocky is the fourth to serve in this capacity), who was
instrumental in developing the Oregon Coast Trail in the 1970s and 1980s.
Jack now lives in Bend, and I enjoyed meeting with him there to hear his
recollections firsthand. One serendipitous introduction led to another,
and I was continually amazed at the many people willing to share their
stories or expertise with me. I met with Robert Hadlow, who is a historian
with the Oregon Department of Transportation and an expert on historic
bridges, to pick his brain about pedestrian access on McCullough bridges.
As a result, I better appreciated walking across them. A number of OPRD
staff met with me so I could learn more about how they protect and manage our beaches. Some personally accompanied me on parts of the OCT.
I met as well with staff from the Siuslaw National Forest about their role
in managing the Oregon Dunes National Recreation Area. Joanne Kittel
and Jesse Beers spoke with me at length about the history of Amanda's
Trail on Cape Perpetua. Thank you to Al LePage, a tireless advocate for

the trail for twenty years, who participated in developing the Sawmill & Tribal Trail and first brought it to my attention. I enjoyed meeting with Matt Love over coffee in Astoria to talk riprap. I appreciate the time that staff and advocates from other states took to talk with me about coastal issues they face.

Some of my research involved visits to special libraries, history centers, or archives. Thank you to staff, librarians, and archivists at the Oregon State Archives, Western Oregon University, University of Oregon Special Collections & University Archives, Oregon State Library, National Archives at Seattle, Multnomah County Library, Lincoln County Historical Society, Coos Historical & Maritime Museum, Tillamook County Historical Society, and Cannon Beach History Center and Museum. All were extremely helpful and responsive to my requests for information, but a special shout-out should go to Laura Wilt with the Oregon Department of Transportation, Julie Osborne with the Oregon Parks and Recreation Department, and Scott Daniels with Oregon Historical Society.

Jon, Dan, Corinna, and Kirk—the Cartesian Brothers Collective— worked magic with GPS data I generated from many hikes and converted them into readable and useful maps. They were able to unscramble my mistakes, and from the beginning, they showed great enthusiasm for this project.

Chris Carlson, Joy Rhodes, John Hoffnagle, Joanie Campf, and Jane Comerford all read early drafts of this manuscript and offered extremely helpful comments and suggestions. Alix Smith helped out with her amazing photo-editing capabilities.

My happiest memories have been, and always will be, of times spent at the Oregon Coast with family and friends, where we've celebrated anniversaries, reunions, birthdays, reading group gatherings, and other special events—all punctuated with long walks on the beach. Thank you all for sharing my enthusiasm and supporting my passion by joining me along the trail as I experimented with high- and low-tide alternatives and otherwise tried to make sense of it all. It made the journey so much fun!

And a special thanks to Craig and Joy, the best companions of all along the trail.

Sources

Books and Other Publications

Chester H. Armstrong, *Oregon State Parks History, 1917–1963*, Oregon State Highway Department, 1965

Steven Astillero, *Lighthouses of Oregon: A Pictorial Guide*, Nature's Design Photography, 2005

Gunter P. Barth (Editor), *All Quiet on the Yamhill: The Civil War in Oregon, the Journal of Corporal Royal Bensell*, University of Oregon Books, 1959

Stephen Dow Beckham, *The Indians of Western Oregon: This Land Was Theirs*, Arago Books, 1977

———, *The Simpsons of Shore Acres*, Arago Books, 1991

Joe R. Blakely, *Lifting Oregon Out of the Mud: Building the Oregon Coast Highway*, CraneDance Publications, 2006

———, *Oswald West: His Life and Legacy*, CraneDance Publications, 2012

David E. M. Bucy and Mary C. McCauley, *A Hiker's Guide to the Oregon Coast Trail: Columbia River to Tillamook Bay*, Oregon State Parks and Recreation Branch, 1977

Robert Clark, *The Solace of Food: A Life of James Beard*, Steerforth Press, 1993

Jane Comerford, *At the Foot of the Mountain: An Early History of Manzanita, Classic Ridge and Neah-Kah-Nie*, Dragonfly Press, 2004

Thomas R. Cox, *The Park Builders: A History of State Parks in the Pacific Northwest*, University of Washington Press, 1988

Samuel N. Dicken, *Pioneer Trails of the Oregon Coast*, Oregon Historical Society, 1971

Nathan Douthit, *The Coos Bay Region 1890–1944: Life on a Coastal Frontier*, Coos County Historical Society, 2005

————, *A Guide to Oregon South Coast History: Traveling the Jedediah Smith Trail*, Oregon State University Press, 1999

Judy Fleagle and Richard Knox Smith, *Crossings: McCullough's Coastal Bridges*, Pacific Publishing, 2011

Laura O. Foster, *Portland Hill Walks: 24 Explorations in Parks and Neighborhoods*, Timber Press, 2013

R. J. Guyer, *Douglas County Chronicles, History from the Land of One Hundred Valleys*, The History Press, 2013

Robert W. Hadlow, *Elegant Arches, Soaring Spans*, Oregon State University Press, 2001

Bonnie Henderson, *Exploring the Wild Oregon Coast*, The Mountaineers, 1994

————, *120 Hikes on the Oregon Coast*, The Mountaineers, 2004

Charles K. Johnson, *Standing at the Water's Edge: Bob Straub's Battle for the Soul of Oregon*, Oregon State University Press, 2012

Richard W. Judd and Christopher S. Beach, *Natural States: The Environmental Imagination in Maine, Oregon, and the Nation*, Resources for the Future, 2003

Matt Love, *Grasping Wastrels vs. Beaches Forever Inc.*, Nestucca Spit Press, 2003

Lewis Mcarthur, *Oregon Geographic Names*, Oregon Historical Society Press, 1992

Lawrence C. Merriam Jr. and David G. Talbot, *Oregon's Highway Park System 1921–1989: An Administrative History*, Oregon Parks and Recreation Department, 1992

Kenn Oberrecht, *Oregon Coastal Access Guide: A Mile-by-Mile Guide to Scenic and Recreational Attractions*, Oregon State University Press, 2008

Emil R. Peterson and Alfred Powers, *A Century of Coos and Curry*, Binford & Mort, 1952

Jack D. Remington, *The Oregon Coast Trail: Hiking Inn to Inn*, Maverick Publications, 2005

Alexandria Ley Rock, *History of Little Nestucca Country*, Tillamook County Historical Society, 2007

Dwight A. Smith, James B. Norman, and Pieter T. Dykman, *Historic Highway Bridges of Oregon*, Oregon Historical Society Press, 1989

Kathryn A. Straton, *Oregon's Beaches: A Birthright Preserved*, Oregon State Parks and Recreation Branch, 1977

William L. Sullivan, Hiking Oregon's History, Navillus Press, 1999

————, 100 Hikes/Travel Guide: Oregon Coast & Coast Range, Navillus Press, 2009

Ward Tonsfeldt, *Celebrating the Siuslaw: A Century of Growth*, Discover Your Northwest, 2010

Brent Walth, *Fire at Eden's Gate: Tom McCall and the Oregon Story*, Oregon Historical Society Press, 2000

Bert and Margie Webber, *Bayocean: The Oregon Town that Fell into the Sea*, Webb Research Group, 1992

Don Whereat, *Our Culture and History*, The Confederated Tribes of Coos, Lower Umpqua, and Siuslaw Indians, 2010

Lionel Youst, *She's Tricky Like Coyote: Annie Miner Peterson, an Oregon Coast Indian Woman*, University of Oklahoma Press, 1997

Articles and Other Written Materials

Samuel Boardman, "Oregon State Park System: A Brief History," reprinted from *Oregon Historical Quarterly* LV, no. 3, September 1954

R. Scott Byram, "Shell Mounds and Shell Roads: The Destruction of Oregon Coast Middens for Early Road Surfacing," *Current Archeological Happenings in Oregon* 34, no. 1, 2009, http://works.bepress.com/cgi /viewcontent.cgi?article=1001&context=byram

Congressional Record, Proceedings and Debates of the 86th Congress, Second Session, January 25, 1960

Sheila de la Rosa, "Reconstructing a Historic Retreat," *Oregon Home Magazine*, Fall 1999, http://richelstromconstruction.com/wp-con tent/uploads/2011/02/OswaldCabin-OregonHome.pdf

John Dellenback Papers, 1964–2000, Special Collections and University Archives, University of Oregon Libraries

Samuel Dicken, "A Hiking Trail the Length of the Oregon's Coast?" *Old Oregon Magazine* of the University of Oregon Alumni Association, August–September 1959

Mason Drukman, "Oregon's Most Famous Feud: Wayne Morse versus Richard Neuberger," *Oregon Historical Quarterly* 95, no. 3, Fall 1994

Dennis Griffin, "The Evolution of Oregon's Cultural Resource Laws and Regulations," *Journal of Northwest Anthropology* 43, no. 1, 2009

Frank Herbert and Beverly Herbert, Interview by Willis E. McNelly, California State Fullerton, English Department, February 3, 1969, http://www.sinanvural.com/seksek/inien/tvd/tvd2.htm

Joanne Kittel and Suzanne Curtis, "Early Yachats History: The Yachats Indians, Origins of the Yachats Name, and the Reservation Years," 1996, revised 2010

Joanne Kittel, The Amanda Trail Story, 2013, http://www.yachats.info/history/Amanda_Trail.html

Janet McClellan Papers, 1966–1972, Western Oregon University Archives

National Coast Trail Association, Oregon Coast Trail: Missing Links, Priorities & Solutions; Opportunities for Discussion & Action with Public Agencies and Landowners, 2005

Maurine and Richard L. Neuberger Papers, 1954–1966, Oregon Historical Society Research Library

Oregon Blue Book 2013–14, Oregon State Archives, Office of Secretary of State

Oregon Coastal Management Program, "Coastal Zone Management Act Section 309, Assessment and Strategy 2011–2015", prepared for Office of Ocean and Coastal Resources Management, National Ocean & Atmospheric Administration

Oregon Department of Transportation History Committee, "Oregon on the Move, a History of Oregon's Transportation Systems," 2009

Oregon Parks and Recreation Department, Oregon Shore State Recreation Area Rules, Oregon Administrative Rules, Division 21 Rules with Certain Division 4, 24 & 30 Rules, 2013

Guy and Barbara Reynolds, "The Joy of Hiking Along Oregon Beaches," *Oregon Motorist Magazine* October 1929–June 1930

David Schaper, "N.J. Spars Over Free Beach Access Post-Sandy," *Superstorm Sandy: Before During and Beyond*, National Public Radio, December 12, 2012

Surfrider Foundation, NaturalEquity, and EcoTrust, "Non-Consumptive Ocean Recreation in Oregon: Human Uses, Economic Impacts & Spatial Data," 2011

Robert William Straub Papers, 1970–2003, Western Oregon University
   Archives

Oswald West, "Oregon Owns Her Beaches," *Oregon Motorist Magazine*,
   May 1930

William Yardley, "Terrible Tillie, Where the Departed Rest Not Quite in
   Peace," *New York Times*, October 24, 2007

Films

Politics of Sand, a film by Tom Olsen, Jr., a Cannon Beach History Center
   Production, 2009

Oregon Legends: The John Dellenback Story, a Production of Southern Oregon
   Public Television, 2004

Interviews

John Allen, Coastal Region Manager, Oregon Parks and Recreation Department

Carl Bauer, Deputy Ranger, Central Coast Ranger District, ODNRA,
   Siuslaw National Forest

Jesse Beers, Cultural Director, Confederated Tribes of Coos, Lower Umpqua,
   and Siuslaw Tribes

Claude Crocker, District Manager, Central Coast, Oregon Parks and
   Recreation Department

Ernest Drapela, former Chair, Oregon Recreation Trails Advisory Council

Una Glass, Executive Director, Coastwalk California

Dennis Griffin, State Archaeologist, State Historic Preservation Office,
   Oregon Parks and Recreation Department

Robert Hadlow, Senior Historian, Oregon Department of Transportation

Rocky Houston, State Trails Coordinator, Recreation Programs, Oregon
   Parks and Recreation Department

Gerry Hutson, Ownership Specialist, Oregon Department of State Lands

Joanne Kittel, Author and Yachats Resident

Chris LaCosse, Recreation Staff, Central Coast Ranger District, ODNRA,
   Siuslaw National Forest

David N. Land, Attorney at Law, Director, Coastal Law Team, Legal
   Services Division Texas General Land Office

Al LePage, Executive Director, National Coast Trail Association

Linda Locklin, Coastal Access Program Manager, California Coastal Commission

Matt Love, Author and Astoria Resident

Nancy Nelson, State Parks Archaeologist, Oregon Parks and Recreation Department

Ryan Parker, Central Coast Beach Ranger, Oregon Parks and Recreation Department

John Potter, Assistant Director, Park Operations, Oregon Parks and Recreation Department

Jenny Price, Visiting Professor of Environment and the Humanities, Princeton University

Joni Quarnstrom, Public Affairs Officer, Siuslaw National Forest

Jack Remington, former Trails Coordinator, Oregon Parks and Recreation Department

Calum Stevenson, Coastal Coordinator, Oregon Parks and Recreation Department

Tim Strickler, Aquatic Resources GIS Unit Lead, Washington Department of Natural Resources

Index

Page numbers in *italics* refer to pages with images.
Maps are indicated with the letter *m*.

About the Author

Connie Soper first visited Oregon's beaches as a child when she lived in Coos Bay, and she has loved them ever since. She first hiked the Oregon Coast Trail in its entirety over three summers, 2006 to 2008, with many friends and family members. As an active hiker and a former transportation planner, this project was natural for her. She intends to continue walking it forever and to advocate for making improvements to the OCT so that future hikers will be able to experience a fully developed trail. She divides her time between Portland and Manzanita.